Mary Emmerling's
American Country
SOUTH

Mary Emmerling's
American Country
SOUTH

Text by Carol Sama Sheehan
Photographs by Langdon Clay

CLARKSON N. POTTER, INC./PUBLISHERS
NEW YORK

For my mother, who was born in Virginia.
For my dad, who was born in Alabama.
And to everyone in my family, but
Especially for Samantha and Jonathan, always.

Design by Gael Towey
Assisted by Deborah DeStaffan

Photographs on pages 166–171 are by Tina Freeman,
and on pages 266–275 by Chris Mead.

Published by Clarkson N. Potter, Inc., 201 East 50th Street,
New York, New York 10022
and distributed by Crown Publishers, Inc.

CLARKSON N. POTTER, POTTER, and colophon are trademarks
of Clarkson N. Potter, Inc.

Manufactured in Japan

Library of Congress Cataloging-in-Publication Data

Emmerling, Mary Ellisor.
Mary Emerling's American country South/text by Carol Sama
Sheehan; photographs by Langdon Clay.
p.   cm.
Includes index.
1. Interior decoration—Southern States.   2. Decoration and ornament,
Rustic—Southern States.
3. Southern States—Social life and customs.   I. Sheehan, Carol Sama.
II. Title.   III. Title: American country South.
NK2002.E47   1989   747.215—dc19   88-36974
ISBN 0-517-56175-1
10 9 8 7 6 5 4 3 2 1
First Edition

Acknowledgments

This book owes its first debt to all of my friends in the South. From them I learned that Southern hospitality still thrives. They opened their doors and their hearts to me and always gave their enthusiastic support. So to them, a special thanks for adding their Southern spirit to my efforts.

Two friends in particular contributed their knowledge of Southern history and their expertise in opening doors for me in the South: Bobbie King of Jackson, Mississippi, who showed me the wonders of her home state; and Deanne Levison of Atlanta, Georgia, who has a love of antiques, especially those from the South, and who shared what she knew.

I would like to thank everyone who participated in making this book a special one for me:

In Alabama: The late David Hand and his wonderful children, Matt and Shonda; Walter and Patricia Greiss; Michael Leventhal and Ann Sieller and the Mobile Historic Development Corporation; Tom Porter of the Mobile Area Chamber of Commerce; Delaine and Joe Ray; and Mary Swayze and her husband, Roy, who will be terribly missed.

In Florida: Everyone at the Audubon House, Key West; Chris and Stacy Childs; Bill Conkle and Tony Falcone; Robert Davis and Nancy Patrie of Seaside; Mary Fitzpatrick and everyone at the Thomas Edison Home; Nancy Jameson and Molly Wylli at the Wrecker's Museum, Key West; Aix and Peggy Kappel; Holly and Stephen Meier; and Jayne Rice and Richard Vandenbosch at Bonnet House.

In Georgia: A.B. and Nancy Albritton, especially for their potluck supper; everyone at the Atlanta Historical Society; Pat and Rip Benton, and everyone at the Old Edward's Inn; James and Nancy Braithwaite; Faith Brunson; Bob and Julia Christian; Dr. and Mrs. Keith Dimond; Clare and Wiley Ellis; Jodi and Pat Holmes; James Kirkland and Frank; Bobbie and Norman Larson; Jane Symmes and Jeanne Symmes; Betsy Taylor; and Bettye and John Wagner.

In Kentucky: Larrie Currie; Ed Nickels; Jim and Mary Oppel; all the people at Shaker Village at Pleasant Hill; Alexander Speer; and Shelly Zegart.

In Louisiana: Andre and Warren Kenneth Carter; Tina Freeman; the McIlhenney Tabasco Company, especially Paul C.P. McIlhenney, and the people at Avery Island; Bobby and Katie Johnson; Loree and Richard Meyer; everyone at the New Orleans Junior League Show House; and Ed Newton, whose death in 1988 was a terrible loss.

In Maryland: Doug Cramer; James Cramer and Dean Johnson; John Newcomer; Betty Phillips; Pat Scheibel; and Bill and Ruth Spann.

In Mississippi: James Anderson; Marjorie Anderson; Camp and Suzanne Best; Martha and Wayne Flannigan; Bill and Nancy Grogan; Mr. and Mrs. Jacob Guice; Bobbie and Dub King—again and again; Pat and Wayne Terry Lamar and Lucius; Hammack, Aubrey, and Mulkey at Mammy's Cupboard; everyone at Melrose Plantation, especially Fred; Mimi and Ron Miller; everyone at the Natchez Pilgrimage Tour; Mary Pickard and everyone at Shearwater Pottery; Bill and Sylvia Scott; and Terry Weinberger at the Balfour House.

In North Carolina: Betty and Dick Baker; L.C. and Charlotte Beckerdite; the women in Cameron who have a great antiquing town; Karen Cauble; Marcia Crandall; Jerry Darnell; Charles Duell; Linda Jordan Eure and Sheila Hufton, and everyone at Historic Edenton; David and Mary Farrell of Westmoore Pottery; Gwen and Ron Griffin; Philip and Susan Harvey; David McCall; Marguerite McCall; Darlene and Holland McPeake; Fred and Peggy Smith; and Mary Sparger.

In South Carolina: Jean Aldredge; Susan Bison and everyone at Middleton Place; Charlene Burns; Rosemary Hertel; Jane and Robert Hicklin; Mr. Hiott and everyone at Walnut Grove Plantation; Joyce and Lowrey King; Claire Sasser; Kim Tuck; and Helen Turner.

In Tennessee: Dr. and Mrs. Ben Caldwell; John C. Holtzapple of the James K. Polk Home; and Salli and Welling LaGrone.

In Virginia: Jim Eroves of V.W. Jones & Co—the best Smithfield hams; Linda Goldstein and the people at Woodlawn Plantation; Hermen and Monica Greenberg; Mary and Peter Gustafson; Irma Hariton; Mr. and Mrs. Jameson and the people at Berkley Plantation; Bill Jenkins and Dennis Owen; Dr. and Mrs. Fred Laughon; Ms. Nel Laughon; Bettie and Seymour Mintz; and Ron and Sandi Resnick.

And in Washington, D.C.: Carolyn and Myles Doherty; Rae Koch and the staff at the Old Stone House; and Marston Luce and Julie Southworth.

Thank you, Mother, for teaching me all about Southern manners and hospitality, a legacy I now share with my own children.

To my brothers, Terry and Steve, in Washington, D.C., and my sister, Nancy, in Alabama, who love the South as I do.

And always, to my children, Samantha and Jonathan, who gave me the time to do another book.

To Juanita Jones—again—for helping me stay on the road.

To Chris Mead, who worked on our vacation to do our home in Key West—a big ♥

To Pamela Reycraft, who worked so hard on this book.

To Langdon Clay, who photographed this beautiful book and taught me so much about the South.

To Gayle Benderoff and Deborah Geltman, for all their support and their time on each and every book.

To my new editor at Clarkson N. Potter, Lauren Shakely—I hope this is the first of many collaborations.

To all the people at Crown Publishers who make these books possible: Alan Mirken, Bruce Harris, and Carol Southern.

To Gael Towey, who designed the most wonderful Southern, romantic book I have ever seen. Thank you for all of the hours, days, and weeks you took to make the photographs come alive.

To Anne DeVault, Deborah DeStaffan, Amy Boorstein, and Joan Denman, for all of their hard work.

To Hilary Bass, for all of her help.

To Jody Grief, who helped—again!

My special thanks and appreciation go to the network of country friends all over the United States—without you there would be no books.

To all of you: keep your hearts and your doors open to all of your friends!

Contents

Introduction

Like all Southerners, I care passionately about the South—its people, its landscape, and its old-time customs. When I was growing up in and around Washington, D.C., and spending my vacations and holidays at the family cottage on the beach in Maryland, being Southern meant relaxing with family and friends over the Christmas holidays, enjoying crabs and lobster around a big table on the Fourth of July, rocking on the front porch as the fireflies flickered on a June evening, and horseback riding on the beach by the ocean just as the dogwoods burst into bloom in the spring. Southern memories differ from region to region—Deep Southerners transplanted North may long for Spanish moss and live oaks, folks from bayou country may dream of cypress knees in a lonely swamp, and natives of Kentucky and Tennessee may recall red clay fields and rolling hills—but few Southerners ever feel completely severed from their roots. "Southern accent" and "Southern hospitality" may be clichés, but the warmth those phrases symbolize is still fresh and real in the South today.

One of the reasons the South has so much tradition is that it has a unique position in the country's history. Southerners regard the Civil War—or the "Misunderstanding," as it is sometimes called—as an important part of their region's history: nearly 125 years after the battles ended at Antietam and Shiloh, flowers are still laid on Confederate graves. But Southern history

ABOVE: *The battlefield at Antietam is still a haunting reminder of the bloodiest battle of the Civil War.* LEFT: *Trees planted when the South was young now create stately allees.*

is as old as the first settlement at Jamestown, Virginia, and as young as Cape Canaveral. Whether their affections are with the Old South or the New, Southerners cherish the value of historic events, and they pass on their respect through the generations. As a member of a family that produced two U.S. presidents, William Henry Harrison, the ninth, and Benjamin Henry Harrison, the twenty-third, I never forget the special pride all Southerners have in their heritage.

When I set out on my journey through American Country South, I hardly had to knock on doors—Southerners were on their verandahs ready to invite me inside. In their homes I found the same charm, romance, and all-out friendliness I love in the Southern personality. *American Country South* is about people who have made the joyful discovery that going home again is not only possible—it is the greatest pleasure in life.

"Y'all come back and see us now . . ."

LEFT AND RIGHT: *Berkeley, built in 1726, was home to two presidents, William Henry and Benjamin Harrison, both Mary's ancestors. Today open to the public, it offers beautiful scenes from the distinguished history of the South.*

T he border between Pennsylvania, Delaware, Maryland, and West Virginia, first mapped out in 1763 by surveyors Charles Mason and Jeremiah Dixon to settle a land dispute, has since evolved into

The Mason-Dixon Line

a symbolic border between North and South, giving the South its nickname, Dixie. ★ Although no billboard calls attention to a demarcation, the traveler crossing this line today experiences it as the departure from one world and the entrance into a subtly different one.

Washington, D.C.
Maryland
Virginia

What accounts for the warm formality of the homes of the Colonial South? In the 18th century, rivers were dependable highways to the sea, and nearly as many seagoing vessels made Europe their destination as they did New England. Southern planters built mansions in the Federal or Neoclassical style, complete with urns, eagles, and boxwood hedges, and furnished them with portraits, tables, and chairs crafted in England. Horsemanship in the British tradition was also pursued with zeal. But the South's cultural independence from the North started out as a practical reality—its physical isolation—not as a snobbish rejection. Gentility—American style—still has an important place in the old counties of the Southern border states.

In contrast to the "to the manner born" style found inland, life along the Eastern Shore and the Atlantic has followed a simpler rhythm. In this until now sparsely populated flatland, fishing, oystering, and hunting are not just sports but essential put-food-on-the-table jobs. A few miles down the road from the country gentleman's estate is another side of rural life. Here real folk enjoy the unmanicured splendor of their natural surroundings, and no one uses double-talk to sell his catch of the day.

Yet whether they look out over hills or over marshes, or pull on riding boots or hip boots, the Southerners at the South's northern edge have more in common with each other than with their Yankee neighbors. A less harried pace and a gentle accent in local voices invite the visitor to slow down, take notice, and really listen to what people have to say. No matter how long the work day, Southerners make time for watching a sunset or a flock of migrating birds.

In modern cities and even in suburbs it's easy to forget America's agrarian past. But in the South, remembering the country way of life is second nature, just because there are so many glimpses of it along the road. Cattle and dairy farming—both large- and small-scale—are part of the Southern economy, and there are still thoroughbred estates tucked among the valleys of the Blue Ridge Mountains of Virginia. In fact, the tradition of the gentleman farmer began on Virginia's tobacco plantations in the 17th century, when the colony supplied Europe with the coveted new commodity. Today tobacco farming, though important, is less a part of Virginia's identity than it once was. Instead, the landscapes of Virginia and her sister states are most memorable for patterns of mowed fields and crisscrossing fences, and the gentle haze of a summer morning.

An
Architectural Past

Marston Luce, Washington, D.C.

M arston Luce admits that, as a child growing up in Mobile, Alabama, he was fascinated by its smorgasbord of building types of the Old South. "I'd use an Instamatic camera to 'collect' interesting façades on my walks through different neighborhoods," he recalls.

His love of history and architecture eventually led Marston into the antiques business. He and his partner, Julie Southworth, have assembled in their Washington, D.C., shop an incredible variety of Early American antiques and whimsical 19th-century folk art. His home shows his preference for early 19th-century furniture styles, such as Adam and Hepplewhite, that evoke the classical tradition.

Marston's inspiration may come from many different sources, but his approach to interior design seems very Southern to me. He never "decorates," but instead fills his rooms with objects he

🍂

ABOVE: *Surprising combinations of rustic and refined lend special character to the town house and grounds.* RIGHT: *In the dining room, a Biedermeier side table shelters a monumental Ionic capital. English antler candlesticks illuminate a painting of the Hudson River school. The birdhouse is Maine-crafted.*

LEFT: *Luce's favorite "Edward Hopper" birdhouse stands on a French Empire secretary.* ABOVE: *A tongue-in-cheek addition to the dining room is the 8-foot-high 19th-century pencilmaker's sign.*

ABOVE AND BELOW: *The birdhouse collection continues with a church and a mansard-roofed dwelling with lots of dormers, once an appropriate meeting place for gregarious purple martins.*

ABOVE: *In a small kitchen, mirrored backsplashes make the room seem larger than it is. The scale of unexpected architectural remnants, such as the garden pineapple ornament and the Corinthian plaster mold once used for casting capitals, enhances the illusion.*

collects out of interest and curiosity, and he's not afraid to improvise or to draw on his wonderful sense of humor. He creates unexpected vignettes by juxtaposing, for example, primitive pottery with refined Queen Anne silver. Or he'll set off a large architectural element with the diminutive presence of one of his beloved birdhouses—a passion I also share.

"Birdhouses interest me so much because they're really little buildings," he says, "and it's fun to study them to see how non-professionals solve such architectural problems as roof line or porch supports or window placement."

Marston Luce once considered pursuing a career in architecture, but was put off by graduate schools, which seemed to emphasize the modern glass-and-steel school of building design. His home shows what can be achieved with a sharp eye for classical motifs, and a little tongue-in-cheek.

ABOVE AND BELOW: *Surprises in the living room include a giant pocket watch that originally served as a shop sign.*
FAR LEFT AND LEFT: *An "Old Paris" soup tureen, Queen Anne brass candlesticks, and a pair of Gothic Revival chairs enliven the entry hall with marbleized wood floor.*

Early American Accent

Old Stone House, Washington, D.C.

For me, the romance of the South has a lot to do with its special place in the country's history. Growing up in the Georgetown section of Washington, D.C., I made many school trips to the Old Stone House, the last surviving pre-Revolutionary structure in the District, now maintained by the National Park Service. This building, with its beautiful English gardens, is a reminder of the distinctly Southern traditions of the nation's capital.

Today Georgetown is the most fashionable residential and commercial area of Washington, as well as a historic district. In 1764, when the Old Stone House was built, Georgetown was one of the most important tobacco markets along the Atlantic Seaboard. Its proximity to the plantations of Maryland made it a natural point of inspection and export for the commodity all of Europe craved.

❧

ABOVE AND LEFT: *Locally available building materials, such as bluestone and cedar shakes, give a dormered European-style farmhouse an American accent. In their haste to complete the house, builders arbitrarily left spaces for windows, which accounts for their charmingly irregular sizes and shapes.*

A Pennsylvania German cabinetmaker named Christopher Layman, drawn to the area for its business opportunities, built the six-room house as a residence and workshop. A subsequent owner, Mrs. Cassandra Chew, a widow and a socialite, added a northern wing and fancified its furnishings, but left its feeling of the past intact.

Today the Old Stone House is furnished with household items, both rustic and elegant, typical of a middle-class residence of the 18th century. As a girl, I loved walking through these rooms, softly illuminated by candles or lamps, or by natural light through their small windows. I'm convinced that my preference for small, warmly lit rooms began on my jaunts to this magic place.

LEFT: *In the state-of-the-art carpentry of the day, natural pine floorboards were cut to the length of the dining room. The random paneling used for the walls was brought from an older home in the area. The elegant line of the pilaster was sacrificed to accommodate the cupboard. The William and Mary gateleg table of maple and oak, dated 1689, shows off a setting of Leeds china.*

LEFT: *Two hundred years' worth of layered paint on a bedroom's corner fireplace has been scraped away to reveal the original Colonial-day paint.*
RIGHT: *In the parents' bedroom, rough-hewn pine beds with straw mattresses are made up with homespun spreads. A Shaker-type rocker is strategically located at the "swift," a labor-saving device used to ball yarn.* **BELOW RIGHT**: *A quilling box was used to preshrink thread. As the wheels turned, thread passed through a trough of water, then wound onto a bobbin, shrinking naturally as it dried. Common in the 18th century, this tool is a collector's find today.*

Homespun South

James Cramer and Dean Johnson, Maryland

The farmhouse of James Cramer and Dean Johnson, partners in an antiques business, represents a real hands-on country style of life. The house is filled to the rafters with the crafts and traditions of the rural South. Open cupboards overflow with baskets, herbs hang from the beams to dry, and the dolls that James fashions out of old piece goods and feed sacks populate nearly every room. The textiles the two collect—homespun, calico, bed ticks, and quilts—for me are an overlooked but important piece of our heritage. They recall an era when every article of daily life was made by hand.

James and Dean searched long and hard for this place, where crafts can be pursued without distractions and the precious inventory of 19th-century country life can be displayed as well as collected. As James says, "I wanted the feeling you might get as a kid going over to Grandma's house, a place where you don't worry about setting down a glass without a coaster under it."

❧

LEFT AND ABOVE: *A pair of welcoming country chairs with woven backs needs only visitors to complete a familiar Southern scene. Built in the Federal style in the 1830s, this typical Maryland farmhouse received its Victorian front porch, complete with spindlework columns, brackets, and sawtooth frieze, in the 1870s.*

35

Twig furniture provides a perch for enjoying a variety of other perches. The use of birdhouses to lure birds into the garden is a time-honored method of pest control especially popular in the South. Fashioned from lumber scrap, they are sometimes whimsically designed. ABOVE FAR RIGHT AND BOTTOM FAR RIGHT: With its original tin roof, the smokehouse stands as a reminder of the routines and rituals practiced by earlier homesteaders.

ABOVE: *Time-worn textiles are on view in a living-room cupboard.* LEFT: *Homegrown flowers and herbs brighten the bay-window view. A collection of regional baskets in many shades of green hangs from the original ceiling beams. James Cramer made the dolls on the church bench out of old feed sacks.*
RIGHT: *Ladderback chairs with ice-cream-cone finials surround a three-plank table in front of a fireplace converted into a linen press. On the mantel, a hand-crafted log cabin with authentic chinked walls, the work of Dean Johnson, is landscaped with two makeshift evergreens.*

Although equipped with the conveniences of a modern kitchen and pantry, the heart of the home with its exposed log walls and ceiling beams looks untouched. LEFT: The long-handled basket from Tennessee over the mantel was used on farms to keep important keys in one place.

ABOVE AND BELOW: *Two upstairs bedrooms show off calico dresses, blouses, and bonnets worn by children of an earlier time. The small red-painted "hired man's bed" was once reserved for itinerant farm workers.* RIGHT: *An array of wool blankets includes a navy-and-white coverlet made by John Welty.* FAR RIGHT: *The old milk cupboard holds a collection of mattress tickings, pillowcases, large pieces of homespun, and quilts folded to exhibit their pretty gingham undersides.*

Just South of the Border

John Newcomer, Maryland

John Newcomer's Southern roots run deep. His great-grandfather was appointed Maryland's commissioner of education for the Shenandoah Valley in 1867 by Abe Lincoln. He was also responsible for founding the first black college, in Harper's Ferry, West Virginia, where John himself was born.

"But, you know," he says with a smile, "it takes a long time to be accepted down here. The other day, when I tried to join a discussion on a bit of local history, a neighbor said, 'Oh, John, you wouldn't know about that, you're not even from the South'!"

Maryland historically is a border state with a divided sense of cultural identity. John believes that most people in

🦋

LEFT: *The carved wood finial on the porch once ornamented a Gothic Victorian in eastern Canada.* RIGHT: *Funkstown founders erected this cut limestone structure in about 1780.*

LEFT: *The formal living room includes a wealth of antiques, including a lattice-backed walnut chair, first acquired by the Crow family of Virginia in 1760—the only known surviving example of the American Chinese Chippendale style of garden furniture. The portrait of Isabel Ames of Alfred, Maine, was painted by itinerant artist Jonah Treadwell in 1843.* **ABOVE**: *A carved wooden rooster struts unceremoniously in a swagged window.* **BELOW LEFT**: *Posed before the Album Quilt in the library, the cow weathervane still retains its original gold leaf finish.*

the area where he lives, while lacking Southern accents, have adopted Southern attitudes toward entertaining. "For example, they really like to throw informal events like buffets, picnics, or garden parties," he points out.

His own house is an enthralling blend of old family heirlooms and painted furniture, folk art, and other objects collected throughout the border states.

John first moved to Funkstown, population 1,100, because he loved its tranquil setting and its proximity to so many historic sites, including Antietam, the National Battlefield, site of the bloodiest conflict of the Civil War. It was a nice coincidence that his ancestors happened to be related to the Funk family that founded the town in 1768. If his neighbor knew that, I'm sure she'd finally accept at least this Newcomer as a native!

RIGHT: *The white door and painted tiger maple finish identify this 1820s corner cupboard as a product of cabinetmakers of Lititz, Pennsylvania. It contains chalkware and spatterware made in England for the Pennsylvania market of the day.*

In the Heart of Horse Country

M o n i c a a n d H e r m e n G r e e n b e r g,
V i r g i n i a

Northern Virginia was a hotbed of spies, conspirators, and hostiles from both sides during the Civil War. Today it is genteel horse country, epitomizing the South's affection for the equine breed as perhaps no place else in the region except the Blue Grass State of Kentucky. Thoroughbreds, hunters, and polo ponies all are bred and trained here.

I first got to know this area when I was a student at Southern Seminary College in Buena Vista. On weekends, my roommate, Kay Bentley, and I would love to take off for Middleburg to visit the wonderful little shops, enjoy the country scenery, and take in the sights of the annual Gold Cup steeplechase event, local horse show, or polo match. I was delighted to get reacquainted with this corner of Virginia through Monica and Hermen Greenberg, who spend their weekends at Rutledge, a two-hundred-year-old country house.

"I was hoping to find an old historic house," says Monica, "and Hermen was looking for land suitable for raising thoroughbreds." Their search turned up a property many people might have ignored. "The house looked abandoned," she recalls. "It had been buried beneath decades of whitewash, diseased stones, and unfortunate modern additions. But we discovered it was a building with good bones—a Federal house with an interesting past." Indigenous materials had been used extensively in the original construction, including full-length tree trunks, complete with bark, for roof beams and floor joists.

&

Although dressed up and expanded over the years, first with a Victorian wing (TOP LEFT), then a screened-in porch and breakfast room at the rear (BOTTOM LEFT), Rutledge remains true to its Virginia country heritage. Built about 1800, its foundation and walls are local fieldstone. LEFT CENTER: The elliptical fanlight and pilasters of the front door are common in Federal houses. RIGHT: Brood mares graze in one of the farm's double-fenced paddocks.

LEFT AND BELOW LEFT:
Front and rear parlors offer an eclectic mix of English and American furnishings and examples of faux painting. The owners sought to gather the objects that a worldly Southern family might have accumulated over several generations. Animal portraits, such as the fire screen with needlepoint panel depicting a King Charles spaniel, were popular displays of the pride of ownership.

RIGHT: *The view from a window looks much as it might have one hundred years ago.* **NEXT PAGES:** *The early 19th-century preference for formality is reflected in the paintings and furnishings in the dining room at Rutledge. Over the 1820s pier table hangs a 19th-century American oil painting that suggests how children of well-to-do families mastered their ABCs. The still life over the mantel was painted by a Union soldier, wounded in the Civil War, as a gift for the Southern family that nursed him back to health.*

Stenciling especially commissioned for the original pine floorboards in the central hall draws on the natural patterns of the native dogwood. FAR LEFT: *A generous central hall features an elaborate girandole mirror topped by an American eagle, a popular motif of the Federal period. Its convex glass increased candle-power in pre-electricity days.*

I am impressed with the house's heritage, but even more impressed with the way the Greenbergs have brought the interior of the house to life. To reclaim the derelict, the Greenbergs, with their close friend and collaborator designer Irma Hariton, mustered an array of artisans and craftsmen. Today, Rutledge stands transformed not merely into a collection of museumlike rooms but a sensitive re-creation of a real home from another century. The couple filled the home with an eclectic mix of furnishings that a worldly Southern family might have accumulated after occupying the same house for several generations. Room after room, the Greenberg house provides a fascinating glimpse into the world of the Virginian of means.

ABOVE LEFT: *The bedroom wallpaper is a reproduction of an early 19th-century floral pattern.* FAR LEFT AND LEFT: *Bathrooms have taken on the guise of the Edwardian era, thanks to wood-frame mirrors, sconces, and antique cabinets fitted with porcelain sinks and onyx counters.* RIGHT: *Artwork framed by glass decorated with eglomise, the technique of reverse painting and gilding on glass, complements a dressing table laid out with sterling silver brushes and crystal vessels.*

A portrait of a grande dame cohabits the parlor nook with an Empire chair, an English table, and an Irish crystal vase. LEFT: The sitting room off the master bedroom has an English needlepoint rug and German Biedermeier birch veneer desk, complete with secret compartments. A Queen Anne mirror with striking carved detail dominates the other wall.

ABOVE: *The small upper rooms at Rutledge derive their character from such details as this window valance, handstenciled with fruits and flowers.*

RIGHT: *The collection of American bonnets in the guest room includes models similar to those worn by pioneer women. The ruffle trim offered sunburn protection.*

RIGHT: *The Album Quilt on the bed, dated 1840, is the work of numerous gifted quilters in the Baltimore area. The English washstand is properly equipped with pitcher and bowl. Now electrified, the bedside lamp was once fueled with oil.*

Rebuilt in its original style, the porch on the back of the house looks as if it has always belonged on the homestead. Victorian wicker furniture provides comfortable seating for surveying the farm. Neatly trimmed topiary, ferns, and floral arrangements give it a conservatory feeling.

ABOVE: *A casual breakfast room, an extension of the porch, features a variety of country pieces, a large hooked rug, and folk paintings of barnyard animals.*

ABOVE AND BELOW: *Handpainted decoration adds a note of rustic charm to ordinary furnishings, whether tin tray and breadbasket or table, chair, and combed-pattern floor.*

Island Retreat

Ruth and Bill Spann, Virginia

A retreat from the honky-tonk and uproar of the boardwalk and the city"—that's what Bill and Ruth Spann call their cozy, uncluttered farmhouse on Chincoteague Island in Virginia. "The first Easter weekend we spent here we walked a nature trail," recounts Bill. "In the space of an hour we saw wild ponies, sika deer, whitetail deer, ducks, quail, and Canadian geese. It was a morning out of *The Peaceable Kingdom*!"

I first met the Spanns through their antiquing sideline, which they have pursued with another couple, Bill and Judy Borge,

❧

ABOVE AND LEFT: *From the driveway paved with oyster shells to the basket quilt and birdhouse adorning the living room, this home reflects the unvarnished charm of the Chincoteague Bay area of eastern Virginia at the Maryland border.*

for nearly twenty years. They call their team the Packrats because they love, as I do, to prowl through secondhand stores, flea markets, and country auctions. When the Packrats take a booth at an antiques show, it's always full of surprising finds, and that's what I like about their house on the island. Whether it's a funky compote made of marbles and Popsicle sticks, or a colorful rug used as a bedcover, there is always something new or different to entertain the visitor.

ABOVE LEFT: *A former roadside vegetable stand is now a sofa table.* LEFT: *The painting, Hissing Goose, is a tribute to the work of Chincoteague Island's legendary decoy carver, Ira Hudson.*

ABOVE: *Shenandoah Valley baskets grace a grain-painted, chip-carved shelf made by a Susquehanna River Valley craftsman.* FAR LEFT: *On the bed is a traditional Canadian "bed-rug" from the 1930s.* LEFT: *The Packrats ingeniously recycled a piece of house trim as a headboard.* BELOW LEFT: *The floor runner is a New Hampshire–made rag rug.*

Hunt Country Weekend

Sandi and Ron Resnick, Virginia

Artist Sandi Resnick and her husband, Ron, are recent transplants to the South, but you would think they had lived there forever. They feel at home not only in their wonderful 1920s fieldstone house, but also in the hunt country of northern Virginia, where the virtues of civility and neighborliness are still practiced. One family lets Sandi pasture her quarter horses, Chinook, Gift of Fire, and Ready, on their land. Another neighbor has been a source of an untold number of fresh vegetables and herbs, as well as inspiring ideas on how best to use them in cooking. My last weekend with the Resnicks was a relaxing mix of good conversation, inventive fare from the kitchen, and all the other comforts of the country.

Although only an hour's drive from Baltimore and Washington, the village of Purcellville has retained its rural character. When I drove through the countryside, recalling my own growing up in a similar world, I felt my newfangled city ways melt away. The Quaker aesthetic adds a touch of elegance to buildings in these agrarian surroundings. That's not to say there's anything sleepy about the region. Horse farms and antiques shops are plentiful and full of activity. Polo matches add excitement and draw tailgaters from all around. Almost everyone has a garden . . . or a good neighbor who has one.

A farm girl from Washington State, Sandi spent many years in California before moving to Virginia, and she hasn't forgotten her West Coast past. "I love preparing a Williamsburg-style Thanksgiving or Christmas dinner for friends and relatives, but guests also expect me to have some California appetizer or entrée mixed in with the traditional menu."

❧

FAR LEFT: *The formal entry of a Georgian side-gabled house is softened by a teakettle bouquet and the household greeter, Scruffie. The tin roof has wrought-iron "snow eagles" to prevent occasional snow from piling up.* ABOVE, CENTER, AND BELOW LEFT: *In the cutting garden, breakfast is a family tradition, with Ron's French toast on Sandi's hand-painted plates.*

ABOVE, LEFT, AND BELOW: *Virtually all of Virginia is horse country, as the paddock of quarter horses, spring foals, and fenced pasture near Leesburg attest.*

Sandi's entertaining style is casual with a flair. "The element of surprise is important to me," she says. "I use antiques, baskets, china, old grain boxes, or toolboxes as serving pieces, and I'm always lavish with herbs and greens."

Like her primitive canvases, Sandi's home is cozy, good-humored, and full of Americana. In her work, she draws on the everyday happenings of the Virginia countryside for inspiration, using farm animals, stone fences, and local architectural treasures like her own home to round out her colorful version of the South.

Neighbor Mary Gustafson is Sandi's source for the freshest herbs and vegetables in all seasons; the first yields of a Southern garden come as early as late spring.
LEFT: *On a rustic table, lavender, lamb's ear, and sage, freshly harvested and dried, are the principal ingredients in homemade potpourri.*
ABOVE: *Tarragon, opal basil, and rosemary vinegars.* **RIGHT:** *Views of Mary Gustafson, her garden, and surrounding fields, with a 1949 red Ford Workmaster tractor.*

Sandi Resnick's Sausage Pie

❦

Lunch with Sandi and Ron Resnick means a mouth-watering meal that can be prepared ahead of time—leaving more of the morning to spend outdoors with the horses! Sandi serves her sausage pie with spicy jalapeño bread and a fresh green salad.

- 1 10-inch pie shell, partially baked and cooled
- 1 pound ground sausage meat (Sandi uses Jimmy Dean sage flavor)
- ⅓ cup chopped onion
- 1 tablespoon butter
- ¾ cup milk
- 1 3-ounce package cream cheese
- 3 eggs
- 1 cup shredded cheddar cheese
- ½ teaspoon salt (use less if your sausage meat is very salty)
- ½ teaspoon Worcestershire sauce
- ⅛ teaspoon pepper

Preheat oven to 375°F. In a heavy frying pan, crumble sausage meat with a fork. Sauté thoroughly, drain fat from pan, remove sausage meat and set aside.

In another frying pan, sauté onions in butter until tender. Add milk and heat until steam rises, but do not boil. Cut cream cheese into small pieces, add to hot milk and onion mixture, and let soften off the stove.

Beat eggs, then add shredded cheddar cheese, milk mixture, and seasoning. Beat to mix thoroughly and pour into pie shell. Top with cooked sausage. Bake 30 minutes or until set.

serves **6** to **8**

FAR LEFT AND BELOW:
For a potluck lunch, the two-board-top tavern table and countrified Windsor chairs are fittingly Southern furnishings, as is an open-at-the-neck dress and pass-the-salt-please style.
LEFT: *The herbal tieback is a typically inventive Southern variation of an old English theme. Bundled delphinium, lamb's ear, sage, oregano, and yarrow give elegance to the curtained window and freshness to the room with every breeze.*

A ticking and quilt transform a rustic chaise lounge into a comfortable perch in the typically Southern sitting room. RIGHT: *Jacquard coverlets and other antique bedcovers are part of Sandi's hand-picked collection.* BELOW RIGHT: *Sandi's hand-painted firescreen features a rural landscape in bold colors.*

The South
in Silhouette

Helen, Nel, and
Dr. Fred T. Laughon, Jr.,
Virginia

A Christmas card caught in time—that's how Cheswick, the home of the Laughon family of Richmond, Virginia, strikes a visitor during holiday season. In December, this 18th-century center-hall Colonial fairly glows with the spirit of American Christmas Past. It is one of the few buildings to survive the conflagrations inflicted on Richmond during the Civil War. Today its tradition-minded owners treat every holiday as a chance to show off the house in appropriately Southern seasonal garb.

The Laughons are a fascinating clan. Dr. Fred T. Laughon, Jr., a retired Baptist minister, and his wife, Helen, are both native Richmonders with roots here dating back two centuries. Helen and daughter Nel make up a team of nationally acclaimed sil-

❧

ABOVE AND LEFT: *Wreaths of boxwood gathered from the Virginia woods, ivy topiaries in terra-cotta pots, and garlands of Virginia Winesap apples adorn the house and studio at Christmastime.* LEFT CENTER: *The lamppost sign is the work of Dr. Laughon.*

ABOVE: *In the studio, the process of silhouetting is artful yet remarkably simple. Helen arranges the subject in profile before a lighted screen, while Nel centers the image.*

ABOVE: *The* camera obscura *was made by Fred Laughon after an original at Monticello.* BELOW: *Once traced, the profile must be cut with special scissors.*

houette artists who work out of a one-room cottage behind their home. The cottage itself is a wonderful curio, having been brought here from nearby Midlothian, where it once functioned as a post office.

History buffs and conservationists, the Laughons bought the 1796 dwelling in 1973 to save it from being swallowed up by an office complex. Moving it to a nearby site, they updated the building's utilities but left untouched all its original features, including the eight fireplaces, heart-pine floors, batten doors, and mortise-and-tenon hand-pegged construction. Besides locating a number of the antiques that enhance the interior of the house, Dr. Laughon, a skilled craftsman, also made many of the pieces of furniture found inside and out.

Before the advent of photography, silhouetting was a popular technique for capturing the images of important and beloved figures. Helen Laughon revived her lifelong interest in drawing shadow figures by taking up silhouetting, along with daughter Nel, some sixteen years ago. Now

RIGHT: *The Laughons' worktable is an eye-catching mix of their own work and old silhouettes, collected for inspiration.*

WILLIAM HENRY HARRISON.

the pair travels 30,000 miles a year, lecturing on their art and practicing it at state fairs and crafts shows.

When I visited the Laughons at Christmas, I found a house completely given over to the holiday, both outside and in. The family enjoys giving large open houses and casual dinners. "I'm an American first and a Virginian second," notes Helen. But by remaining faithful to local 18th-century traditions in their choices for food and décor, she, Fred, and Nel help to impart a valued sense of the past to their many friends who visit them at this time. To Helen, being Southern means "having a bigness in your life. It's a style of entertaining that involves reaching out to others from a position of family pride and unity, but also with a strong sense of the larger community."

LEFT: *A holiday sprig tops an antique cutting of William Henry Harrison, the ninth president and Mary's ancestor.*
RIGHT: *Glossy magnolia leaves and pine boughs, evergreen sprigs and poinsettias continue the country Christmas theme indoors. Artist Margaret Kent painted the staircase mural.*

ABOVE: *Panels above the living-room fireplace depict Cheswick in the 18th, 19th, and 20th centuries.* RIGHT: *A Chippendale-style chair.*

ABOVE: *Apples, pinecones, and evergreen are a Christmasy still life on a fireplace mantel that has witnessed nearly three hundred years of holiday observances.* **LEFT AND RIGHT**: *Brass candlesticks and box are warm accents for the holiday décor.*

A portrait of Nel, age seven, executed by Virginia artist Van Jost in the style of the 18th century, oversees the formal dining room. Cupboards on either side of fireplace were hand-rubbed with yellow ochre, then given aqua borders matching Nel's dress. RIGHT: Dried-apricot Christmas trees, embellished with pansies and dried yarrow, are a colorful alternative for the holiday table.

ABOVE: *Posts of antique bedsteads, made from Virginia heart of pine, have been cut to follow the slant of the roof. This original detail, and the one-legged nightstands, are the clever craftsman's answer to furnishing a small space.*

ABOVE: *The four-poster bed with turned posts was made by Fred Laughon for his daughter, Nel, from wood salvaged from the home of Gen. Douglas MacArthur's mother. At the foot of the bed, on top of the antique pine bride's box, sits a camera obscura.*

LEFT: *Watching over the doll's tea party before the fire are an old-fashioned teddy bear and a toy soldier made by Nel Laughon from a discarded staircase banister.*

Plantation Living

Woodlawn Plantation, Virginia

"A most beautiful site for a Gentleman's Seat," declared George Washington of the 2,000 acres of which Woodlawn Plantation is the centerpiece. The property was Washington's gift to his favorite nephew, Major Lawrence Lewis, and Eleanor (Nelly) Parke Custis, the granddaughter of Martha Washington, on the occasion of their marriage in 1799. The mansion was duly constructed (after a Georgian-style design provided by Dr. William Thornton, the first architect of the U.S. Capitol building) and the Lewis family occupied it for some four decades. Subsequently, it passed through many hands and endured various ups and downs.

❧

LEFT: *More elaborate than most Georgian buildings of the day, Woodlawn has a pedimented gable, Palladian window, and fan window.* RIGHT: *The central hallway received guests by land and by river.* NEXT PAGES: *Woodlawn comes alive at Christmas.*

Today, Woodlawn has been restored to its early 19th-century glory, never more radiant than at Christmastime.

As a schoolgirl living in nearby Georgetown, I used to stop by Woodlawn every December. I still find that visiting historic homes is a wonderful way to collect new ideas for celebrating the holidays.

I particularly like the way Woodlawn uses what it has, rather than bringing in new decorations and ornaments. Greenery gathered on the grounds is fashioned into oversize garlands and swags that truly create an impact. And l love the boxwood "kissing balls," hung in doorways —the 19th-century equivalent of our mistletoe.

Woodlawn truly reflects the customs and personality of its most notable hostess, the charming "Nelly," of whom one visitor, obviously from the North, wrote in 1817:

"She is a great favorite . . . in addition to her brilliant acquirements she is a pattern of every domestic virtue and an excellent housekeeper.

RIGHT: *Sprigs of evergreen add the spirit of the season to portraits in the music room, the 19th-century equivalent of a family room or den. Nelly herself embroidered the firescreen.*

Martha Washington's Great Cake

❧

Handed down to Nelly Lewis by her "Beloved Grandmama," this recipe for a rich white fruitcake is still prepared at Woodlawn every Christmas.

     1 pound sultanas
    15 ounces currants
     8 ounces orange peel, cut in thin strips or coarsely grated
     6 ounces lemon peel, cut in thin strips or coarsely grated
     8 ounces candied citron
     3 ounces candied angelica
    ½ cup brandy, or more if needed
     2 cups sugar
     1 pound butter, brought to room temperature
    10 eggs, separated
     2 teaspoons lemon juice
    4½ cups flour, sifted with 1 teaspoon mace and ½ teaspoon nutmeg
    ⅓ cup sherry
     3 ounces candied red cherries
     3 ounces candied green cherries
       Additional brandy for storing

LEFT: *In the dining room, a silver epergne overflowing with magnolia leaves, holly, pine, yarrow, and fresh fruit makes a stunning centerpiece.*

Put sultanas, currants, orange and lemon peel, citron, and angelica in a bowl and cover with brandy. Cover tightly and soak overnight, stirring occasionally. If fruit is very dry, use more brandy and soak for 48 hours.

Preheat oven to 350°F. Use a 10-inch earthenware or iron Turk's head mold, or an 8½-inch round aluminum mold, or 2 large loaf pans. Grease and flour molds or pans.

Add 1 cup of the sugar to softened butter, beating until fluffy. In a separate bowl, beat egg yolks until very light. Add remaining cup of sugar to yolks, beating constantly. Slowly add lemon juice.

Combine butter and sugar mixture with egg yolk and sugar mixture. Alternately add flour and sherry. Add fruit and brandy, and cherries.

Beat egg whites until stiff and shiny but not dry. Fold into the batter.

Pour batter into the mold or pans: for 10-inch mold, to within 1½ inches of top; for 8½-inch mold or loaf pans, to within ¾ inch of top.

Put a pan of water on oven bottom. Bake batter at 350°F. for 20 minutes. Reduce heat to 300°–325°F. and finish baking, 40 minutes for small cakes or 1 hour and 40 minutes for large cake. Cake is done when a straw comes out clean.

Cool on racks. When completely cool, moisten with brandy, wrap well, and store in tins in a cool place. Keeps several months.

MAKES AT LEAST 11 POUNDS

The Southern Frontier

In search of a better life across the frontier, tens of thousands of pioneers poured over the Cumberland Gap in the 19th century. Today, as then, it serves as the gateway to the bluegrass fields and wooded hills of Kentucky and Tennessee. Tobacco, cotton, soybeans, hogs, poultry, sheep, and cattle are the mainstays of the region's economy, but the cash crop that gives natives the greatest sense of pride is the Kentucky thoroughbred.

Crossing the Appalachians by car, it's easy to imagine what it was like for homesteaders who made the same trip in a covered wagon, pulled by a workhorse they too were proud of, not so long ago.

Kentucky ★ *Tennessee*

Captured in idyllic portraits or real-life settings, the beauty of the Southern frontier owes much to its soaring peaks and rolling river valleys. An unpretentious agrarian culture, clean as mountain air, has grown and thrived here, with crafts handed down through the generations, a rustic counterpoint to the treasure of civilized life "in town."

Historically, Kentucky and Tennessee have had a strong Southern bias. Following the Revolution, Virginia briefly designated Kentucky as one of its counties. North Carolina once annexed Tennessee and might have tried to hold on to it had it not been for the costly job of protecting settlers from the Indians.

During the Civil War, Nashville was a stronghold of the Confederacy, and today it is still a city with the cultural values of a Richmond or a Williamsburg.

Simple Pleasures

Pleasant Hill, Kentucky

My visit to the restored Shaker village of Pleasant Hill amid the bluegrass meadows of central Kentucky was magical. After a day observing the village's broommakers, joiners, coopers, quilters, and weavers, exploring the bountiful kitchen and herb gardens, and hiking down Shaker Landing Road to the Kentucky River, I slept in a traditionally furnished room in one of the community's typical dwellings.

Pleasant Hill was one of seven villages of the Shakers—the United Society of Believers—to be built in what was at that time a near-wilderness known as "the West." At its peak population in the 19th century, 266 buildings housed nearly 500 "believers" and dozens of crafts and industries. Although many of us think of the Shakers as a New England phenomenon, their influence extended throughout the South far beyond the confines of the scattered villages. So-called trustees of Pleasant Hill, responsible for trading with the outside world, traveled the Ken-

❧

LEFT: *The meetinghouse was Pleasant Hill's spiritual center. Painted white to symbolize purity, it is also a reminder of the Shaker commitment to practicality.* ABOVE AND BELOW: *Farm wagons, fences, and other objects of daily life all demonstrate the uncompromising Shaker aesthetic.*

FAR LEFT: *When buried, the self-effacing Shakers usually were identified only by initials.* BELOW: *The headstone naming Emily Gross was erected after "worldly forces" had begun to interact with the community.*

ABOVE LEFT: *Although unfamiliar with limestone as a building material, the Shakers did not hesitate to quarry it and use it to fashion their handsome workshop building in 1811.* CENTER LEFT: *The 1833 pumphouse with rooftop water-level gauge stands next to the men's bathhouse.* BELOW LEFT: *Atop one of the residential houses at Pleasant Hill, dormer windows opening on hinges made rooftop strolls easy; an elegant balustrade made them safe.*

tucky, Ohio, and Mississippi rivers in flatboats filled with their products, produce, and livestock, venturing as far as New Orleans. There is a real spiritual power to the imagery presented by Pleasant Hill. Shakers believed in celibacy, shared property, and equality between men and women, and their simple life-style determined the spare elegance of their surroundings.

Community members rely largely on hand labor, local materials, and "amateur" training in carpentry and architecture. Yet the edifices are flawlessly designed and sturdily built. Whether the plain interiors of houses and barns or a clothespin, bonnet, or basket, the products of the Shakers radiate light and grace.

During my stay at Pleasant Hill, I was touched reading this entry in a journal (complete with misspellings), remarking on the recently completed construction of a limestone building in 1811:

"The work is done in a plain modist stile," she wrote, adding, "As to the people that live in it, with regard to their faith and obedience, their faculties and zeal, we do not know but that they are equally beautiful as their house."

What a perfect summation of the way all of us would like to live.

ABOVE, LEFT, AND BELOW: *A barrel-vaulted ceiling, arches, fanlights, and wainscoting bring clean lines to living and work spaces. Peg racks, a ubiquitous feature of Shaker rooms, facilitate sweeping.*

With a few modern
conveniences tucked away, this
Shaker kitchen would be
an enviable addition to a country
home today. Cheesecloth
kept bugs out of the case piece
where foodstuffs were stored. The
two-tiered stove doubled
the energy output of the woodpile.

FAR LEFT AND LEFT:
Whether designed for dining,
sleeping, or working, Shaker rooms
express a spare, purposeful,
waste-not outlook that is
as fresh today as it was in the
early 19th century. Community
rules forbade decoration.

Log Cabin
Country

Mary and Jim Oppel, Kentucky

It doesn't look like a log house from the outside, but once you step inside the home of Mary and Jim Oppel, the heritage of the Kentucky frontier is there for all to enjoy. The Oppels are proud of the history and traditions of this rural area east of Louisville (Abraham Lincoln's grandfather was killed by Indians just 5 miles away), and they wanted a home that reflected their pride.

Diligently, the couple salvaged logs, stone, woodwork, and other artifacts from old houses marked for demolition, then assembled the materials themselves to combine the riches of the past with comfortable contemporary touches. The labor of love took them a hard three years to complete, but the result is worth it. "It's a real put-up-your-feet kind of house," Jim says proudly of their achievement.

If the house has a theme, it's the fox hunt. The property lies in the heart of fox-hunt country, and Mary is the third genera-

❧

ABOVE: *Twentieth-century siding clads the dogtrot log house. Wood-mullioned double-glazed windows combine period detail with modern energy efficiency.* LEFT: *An old mock orange tree with its fall-yellow "hedge apples" graces the front yard of a new Old Kentucky Home. Pioneers used the thorny bush as natural cattle fencing.*

117

ABOVE: *The gray fox was run to earth years ago in the annual Long Run Hunt. The rare prints are by Mark Catesby, the naturalist who gave Europe its first glimpse of plant and animal life in the Southern colonies. Arriving in 1720, he traveled extensively through the Carolinas, Georgia, and Florida.* LEFT: *The living room is a pleasing combination of rustic and formal. The extra height of the sideboard, a Kentucky-crafted cherry hunt board, facilitated eating and drinking from the saddle.*

tion in her family to take part in this Americanized English country ritual. But the theme doesn't hit you over the head; rather it is played sparely and selectively with just the right decorative additions.

Even in their use of colors, Mary and Jim have paid sensitive tribute to their location. Throughout the house, they have introduced grays and greens to echo the natural colors of the fields of tobacco, corn, and alfalfa that surround them. To sit in a "new" house and yet feel close to the past—that's quite an achievement, especially for first-time home-owners!

LEFT: *The old poplar floor rescued from an 1850s house is painted with a checkerboard design in colors reflecting the grays and greens of surrounding alfalfa, corn, and tobacco fields. Woodwork in the library adjoining the dining room came from the 1790 Benjamin Washburn house in Shelby County, believed to be the first stone dwelling in Kentucky.*

ABOVE: *A walnut Hepplewhite table, made in Kentucky in 1810, exhibits potted shamrock plants, an old powder horn, and an antique English knife box.*
RIGHT: *Hedge apples make a decorative but inedible centerpiece for the mahogany gateleg table, a Centennial (circa 1876) reproduction of a pair of Sheraton banquet ends. Rush-seated fancy chairs from odd sets date from the early 19th century.*

Collecting
Southern Style

Ben and Gertrude Caldwell,
Tennessee

Ben and Gertrude Caldwell have loved antiques ever since they started collecting them on their honeymoon more than thirty years ago. Both come from longtime Tennessee families, but "Gertrude's family was formal French and mine was Chippendale," Ben declares.

Their Nashville house was built to represent a succession of styles appropriate to a residence of the 18th century. It was a departure from the "six-columned Colonial" each had grown up with, and, as it turned out, the perfect background for exhibiting their William and Mary, Queen Anne, and Chippendale antiques. Whether the finds are 18th-century silver or regional wood furnishings, the Caldwells take delight in their beauty and workmanship, not to mention my favorite aspect of collecting—the fun of discovery.

"I guess we're all in it for the chase," laughs Gertrude. "You know how some men hunt duck? Well, Ben hunts antiques!"

❧

ABOVE AND LEFT: *Outside and in, this Eastern Shore–style house was built to reflect the evolution of an 18th-century home.*
ABOVE FAR LEFT: *In the living room, newly milled raised paneling, true to the era, sets off an impeccable collection of antiques, highlighted by a Massachusetts-made mahogany secretary, circa 1770.*
BELOW FAR LEFT: *In the dining room, the towering breakfront holds an impressive selection of early American and English silver.*
LEFT: *The less formal setting of the family room permits showing off a group of Southern-made jugs.*

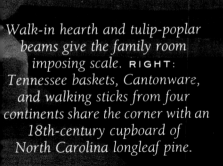

Walk-in hearth and tulip-poplar beams give the family room imposing scale. RIGHT: *Tennessee baskets, Cantonware, and walking sticks from four continents share the corner with an 18th-century cupboard of North Carolina longleaf pine.*

Smoky Mountain Views

Ben and Gertrude Caldwell, Tennessee

Acompound of log cabins in the Cumberland Mountains is the year-round retreat for the Caldwell family.

Bracing swims in spring-fed mountain streams, long walks to waterfalls and overlooks, and reading and talking on porches and swings are the preferred leisure activities here. The Caldwells have also taken the time to befriend and patronize local potters, ironsmiths, coppersmiths, quilters, chairmakers, and basketmakers, treating their products with the same respect and affection as they do their heirlooms and antiques.

The Caldwells frequently invite friends up to the mountains for a taste of informal living. If you're a member of the younger set, chances are you'll pull "pig duty" here some day. That means taking your turn over a 20-hour hickory-wood barbecue, tending a 100-pound dressed pig. The mountain air gives people an appetite, and the Caldwells know just how to satisfy it.

❧

ABOVE: *Built to last, a 19th-century chair still offers a sturdy seat.*
LEFT: *On the deck of a weekend house in the mountains, rockers and a three-seat settee—produced by several generations of a local clan of craftsmen—show a family resemblance.*

127

*Tulip-poplar log cabins from the
1800s, collected from the
area and reconstructed timber
by timber, form a camp
in the woods.*

ABOVE: *Furnished with mountain-made tables and chairs, the living room of the main house is dressed up with an Audubon print and a log cabin portrait in mud and clay.*

ABOVE: *A lazy Susan maple table made in nearby Red Boiling Springs serves hungry hikers.* **BELOW:** *A bedroom with its own fireplace opens onto the deck.*

Plain and Fancy Living

Salli and Welling LaGrone, Tennessee

Every year the Heart of Country antiques and collectibles show is held in Nashville. This former bastion of the Confederacy is still very much a Southern town. Even its rapidly growing suburbs have retained a Southern country tradition.

The middle Tennessee home of Salli and Welling LaGrone, friends I made at the show many years ago, combines the rustic building style of the frontier with the polish and gentility of the Old South's transplanted English aristocracy. It's a home where antiques, regional crafts, and personal collections come together with a special sense of style.

All this was made possible when the LaGrones discovered an old farmhouse in disrepair. They restored it to its original condition, keeping the benefits of modernization, and filled it with

&

ABOVE: The recent addition of a second story has not altered the character of this two-hundred-year-old cabin in the horse country of Middle Tennessee. LEFT: An authentic wilderness interior of chinked logs provides an arresting backdrop for such touches of luxury as Limoges Battersea boxes, a Georgian walnut tea table, and fringed brocade curtains.

ABOVE: *In a living room furnished largely with 18th-century antiques, two framed land deeds signed by Kings George I and William IV and old English tobacco jars bearing the royal warrant pay tribute to the longtime English presence in the culture of the South.*

ABOVE: *Tearing out walls that had concealed the log construction gave birth to a warm and welcoming family room. The split-oak basket on the hearth is by family friend Abraham Lincoln Logsdon.*
LEFT: *A Welsh pine dresser holds a collection of majolica, the 19th-century earthenware noted for its natural shapes and lively color.*

ABOVE: *The baking and preserving traditions of the rural homestead are alive and well in a modern kitchen. Salli LaGrone's well-deserved putation as an excellent cook derives from her skills as a baker and jam maker.*

LEFT AND RIGHT: *Collections of copper molds and Blue Willow dinnerware are displayed in the kitchen and dining room.*

Salli LaGrone's Blackberry Jam

❧

Salli LaGrone, who has studied cooking at Cordon Bleu in France, puts up dozens of jars of her own homemade preserves and jams every year. First-time canners should read about canning in a standard cookbook before trying Salli's recipe. Follow the cookbook or a manufacturer's directions for sterilizing canning jars.

2 **quarts fresh blackberries, washed and picked over**
6 **cups granulated sugar**
  Juice of two medium lemons
⅓ **cup brandy, preferably black-berry**
  3-ounce pouch liquid pectin (Salli uses Certo)

Blend berries and sugar in a nonmetallic pot. (An enameled 6- to 8-quart stockpot is best.) Cook slowly, uncovered, over low heat until the sugar has completely dissolved, about 15 minutes.

Stir lemon juice into sugar syrup, raise heat to high, and bring jam to a boil. Boil for 2 minutes, then stir in brandy. Bring to a vigorous rolling boil that can't be stirred down, and let boil for 1 minute. Add liquid pectin, return to a vigorous boil, and boil 1 more minute.

Remove from stove and ladle into hot, sterilized 8-ounce canning jars. Seal as directed and process in boiling water bath for 10 minutes. Label and date. Should keep on shelf for 1 year.

MAKES **6** to **8** jars

the furniture and collectibles they had gathered while living abroad for six years.

Many of their finds from England and Europe are formal in style, but the couple has a way of taking the starch out of things. As a result, every room in their new-old house offers surprising combinations of plain and fancy. "We always look for furniture that can fit into any house we might live in," says Salli. "You have to gather the bits and pieces, then make them your own."

Though many of her favorite things date from an age when English kings made the rules we lived by, Salli's traditions are those of a busy Southern wife and mother. On my last visit, I found her in the kitchen stirring jam on the stove with one hand and rounding up the kids for a fishing trip with the other.

LEFT: *A pretty-in-pink master bedroom comes as a delightful surprise in a house otherwise true to its log-cabin origins. The heart-of-pine four-poster bed was made by South Carolina artist Mike Craig, who collects centuries-old cotton-mill wood to fashion his creations.* NEXT PAGES: *A screened-in porch, an old standby for comfort and relaxation, is furnished with bent-willow chairs made by Tennessee craftspeople John and Deborah Phillips.*

The Deep South

Time doesn't stand still in Dixie, but it doesn't rush past you, either. Alabama and Mississippi, conservative in the best sense of the word, and Louisiana, that exotic sister state with the French acce t, comprise the heart of the Old South. Here some folks still receive their parcel post by riverboat and hear their music live at the local park gazebo. I love the byways of this region, their timeless beauty and their peaceful ways.

Mississippi ★ *Alabama*
Louisiana

A traveler is never far from spiritual or material refreshment in the Deep South. Roadside attractions range from the antic to the inspirational, along with reminders of sacrifice and loss and the ubiquitous "Co'-Cola" sign. Appetizing regional fare served at establishments like Mammy's Cupboard in Natchez might include hashbrowns and grits with the eggs and hush puppies with the burgers.

Old-time Southern religion also has its own unique flavor. The revival meeting—once a feature of rural communities all over this country—still gathers crowds here under big tents in the summertime, while the steeples of traditional white-painted churches remind passersby to focus their thoughts on heaven.

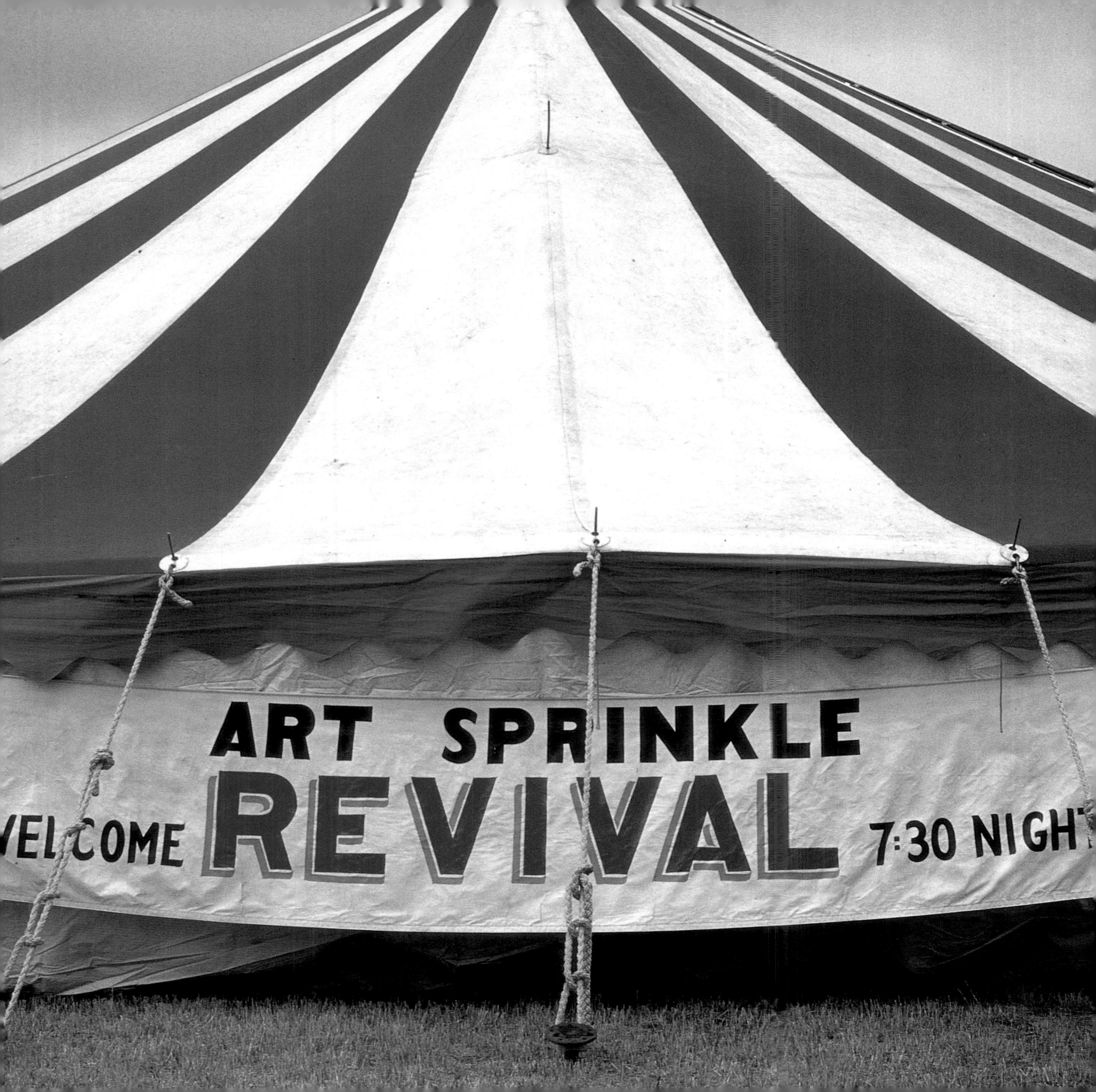
ART SPRINKLE
REVIVAL
VELCOME
7:30 NIGHT

Southerners are family people, with strong ties to kin past, present, and future, and their homes reflect it. A Southern home is lively with the joy of daily events, but it's also a sanctuary for loving memories. Humble family photographs take on a special quality in this setting. Southerners do love their football, especially as played on a Saturday by Ole Miss or the Crimson Tide or LSU. But "homecoming" in the true sense of the word means even more to them. White-railed verandahs, bedsteads festooned with mosquito netting, and a basket of roses are among the simple details that are cherished by those who live in the Deep South. These scenes from Natchez, Mississippi, give a glimpse of the ties that bind the Southern family.

The romance of the South is captured in its architecture, from proud antebellum plantation homes in the country to handsome row houses in town, and in its rich plant and animal life. Fields of cotton in bloom are as picturesque as Spanish moss draped on the limbs of ancient live oaks.

Still, the conventions of Southern homes are as practical as they are charming: deep porches and latticed shutters provide both shade and cooling breezes. In the noonday heat, the whole family may retire to darkened rooms for an hour or two's nap—to arise refreshed for the evening meal. But wit always finds its place alongside wisdom down South. If corn accounts for your prosperity, why not pay tribute with a unique wrought-iron fence?

Back-Country Cabin

Nancy and Bill Grogan, Mississippi

Deep in the woods in the Deep South, Nancy and Bill Grogan have created a home that reflects the rich traditions of Mississippi country as much as it reflects the couple's own tastes and values.

The Grogans relocated the 1830s log cabin to its present site and contributed some subtle landscaping to marry it to its surroundings. When I first saw their transplanted home, I was struck by the setting Nancy had created with contemporary folk art, flowering vines, and split-rail chestnut fencing.

Inside, Nancy's passion for preservation is expressed in the way she combines new and old objects in her converted "animal pen" to narrate faithfully—and wittily—the history of the South.

❧

ABOVE: *A Lady Bank's rose enlivens an old chimney.*
FAR LEFT: *Salvaged from a house in New Orleans, the exterior siding with original gray paint finds a new use in the dining room, as does an old wall reclaimed as heart-of-pine flooring. An old dough bowl contains a pumpkin harvest carved by Lavern Hamberlin.*
LEFT: *The wall cupboard has its original green-over-mustard paint.*

ABOVE AND BELOW: *A Crown of Thorns quilt, the work of Nancy's family, is fittingly framed by an antique quilting loom. The fireboard above the mantel was painted by Nancy Grogan.*

LEFT AND BELOW: *The pencil-post bed of tiger maple is new, but the paddle is an original, still useful for smoothing lumps in the feather mattress.*

Gulf Coast Cottage
with Victorian Charm

Delaine and Dr. Joseph Ray, Alabama

The charming home of Delaine and Dr. Joseph Ray sits in the embrace of three enormous live-oak trees in the historic Oakleigh Garden District of Mobile, only a mile and a half from the heart of the city. The couple have filled the house with family heirlooms, many of which romantically evoke the world of nature. Quilts, plates, and rag rugs show off some of the flowers beloved of Southerners, while lace, needlework, and the appurtenances of the ritual of afternoon tea add a Victorian dimension.

"Old things are often more trouble to live with—they wobble more!" Delaine says. "But we've learned to tolerate their peculiarities because they are so interesting."

Inside and out, the carpenter-Gothic cottage reflects the practical considerations of building on the Gulf Coast a century ago. The house is raised high off the ground to help dissipate the heat and damp of the hot Southern summers. Eleven-and-a-

❧

ABOVE AND FAR LEFT: *Decorative gable trim and the pointed arches and hand-carved railing of the front porch are telltale features of a carpenter-Gothic house built in 1892.* ABOVE LEFT: *From the etched-glass flower-basket pattern on the double doors, the foyer is dominated by romantic floral motifs.* BELOW LEFT: *Shade-loving ivy and impatiens add life to back porch and patio. The handmade bench from an old family dwelling in Mississippi has the same kind of scroll-saw detailing found on the house.*

Framed by the transom arch in the dining room, an antique plate with cabbage roses leads the eye to a trio of majolica plates with a grapevine pattern in the kitchen beyond.

ABOVE: *A salt-glazed stoneware water cooler from England, circa 1900, marks entry to the family room. The original beaded-board walls in the galley kitchen were reproduced in the dining area in the new addition.*

ABOVE: *A 19th-century cypress plate rack from Louisiana displays Wedgwood with a Napoleon ivy pattern.* **BELOW**: *Twin parlors function as living and dining rooms. The framed crazy quilt was made by Delaine's grandmother's aunts.*

half-foot ceilings draw hot air overhead. There is a fireplace in each major room for warmth during the short winter season. The front gallery shades the house, and window shutters filter light and heat and give protection against tropical storms.

The porch, a notably tradition-laden detail, served for welcoming neighbors in the morning, taking naps in the afternoon, and conducting courtships at night. As Delaine points out, "It was like another room of the house in the summertime in the South, and things like the porch swing were essential furnishings."

LEFT: *In the master bedroom, camellias fresh from the garden, Victorian mirrors, and treasured family photographs give a nostalgic Old Southern feeling. One can almost imagine a belle of an earlier era arranging her hair beneath the slow-moving ceiling fan.*

ABOVE: *A lace canopy delicately crowns a Virginia-made four-poster bed of bird's-eye and tiger maples. The rickrack coverlet comes from an old family home in Mobile. The turn-of-the-century needlepoint rug carries on the house's horticultural theme. The quilt by the fireplace, made by the owner's great-grandmother, is embroidered with hearts and state flowers. The bentwood crib, cane-back rocker, and bird's-eye maple armoire all date from the Victorian era.*

Artistry
in Twigs

David Hand,
Alabama

Alabama officials rightly call craftsmen like the late David Hand "the soul of the state." His much-sought-after chairs, tables, and headboards are made of slender willow twigs, carefully bent when still supple and secured to a sturdy frame.

David's father was a maker of willow furniture during the Great Depression, when times were hard, and he dubbed it "hobo art." Although I always admired twig furniture for its rustic looks, David assured me it was also supremely comfortable. He invited me to try out a loveseat—in my favorite heart pattern—"with your hose on." "The only thing between you and nature," he boasted, "will be a few store-bought nails." When David died in 1988, he took a bit of Alabama history with him.

🌿

LEFT AND RIGHT: *David Hand traveled throughout the South scouting for twigs, his favorite being the Alabama willow cut in the early fall for its special golden glow.*

ABOVE: *The parlor owes its opulent wood detailing to the craftsmanship of slaves.*
LEFT: *With its steep-pitched hipped roof, broad galleries, and raised pier construction, this Creole plantation house draws on French, Canadian, and West Indies building traditions.*
RIGHT: *In the plantation office, an 1827 map hangs over the paymaster's desk.*

Southern Hospitality in Grand Style

Magnolia Mound, Louisiana

When Armand Duplantier, aide-de-camp to General Lafayette during the American Revolution, set up his home at Magnolia Mound in 1802, it was a primitive four-room Creole cottage on stilts in the bayous along the Mississippi River.

The aristocratic Armand must not have found fault with his new rustic home or the innumerable hardships offered by the neighborhood—sweltering summers, hordes of mosquitoes, and tropical diseases, to name just a few—because he lived in Louisiana for nearly fifty years.

During that time, he made numerous improvements to house and grounds. He clad the cypress piers of the house with brick.

He plastered the interior walls and fitted the windows with glass. Besides expanding the house, he embellished the rooms set aside for entertaining with classical moldings, carved mantels, French wallpaper, and stately furniture.

Armand needed stamina as well as imagination to reconstruct the fine life he had left behind. Incurably French, he even built a *pigeonnier* to keep his kitchen well supplied with squab.

Like English, Scottish, German, and other settlers elsewhere in the South, this Frenchman brought not only his industry and character to the New World but his taste as well. He may have spent a half-century longing for the civilized existence he had left behind, but he carried more than a touch of civilization to a wilderness frontier.

LEFT: *A Regency-style mirror reflects a "rowing" of Staffordshire cups and saucers, a French custom.* ABOVE RIGHT: *A Sheraton sideboard is set with an English tea service and French cut crystal, all from the early 1800s.* RIGHT: *The multipurpose dining room achieves a unity of theme in the medallion pattern, a popular motif of the time, found in the wallpaper, floor cloth, and chair seats.*

Tina Freeman

ABOVE: *The 17th-century ivory cross and the prie-dieu beside the bed attest to the Roman Catholic heritage of the owner.* LEFT: *Stairs to a finished attic, which was used as sleeping quarters when the house welcomed an abundance of guests.*

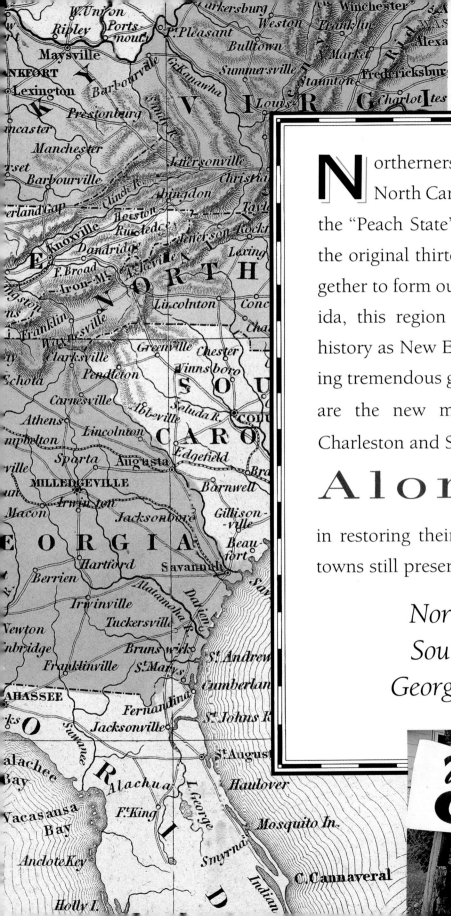

N ortherners sometimes forget that North Carolina, South Carolina, and the "Peach State" of Georgia were three of the original thirteen colonies that came together to form our Union. Along with Florida, this region of the South, as rich in history as New England, is today undergoing tremendous growth. Atlanta and Miami are the new metropolitan centers, and Charleston and Savannah have led the way

Along the Coast

in restoring their own heritage, but small towns still preserve their rural character.

North Carolina
South Carolina
Georgia ★ *Florida*

From Savannah, the old stagecoach route of U.S. 17 winds all the way down the Georgia coast, offering access to the desolate beauty of the beaches and barrier islands on one side, and a rural landscape dotted with small towns and villages on the other. This is not the most glamorous beach scene, but it offers pleasures to be found nowhere else. Wild horses still roam Cumberland Island National Seashore, a thrilling sight. The details of bucolic life—an arrangement of old lawn furniture, a leonine addition to a façade, a neglected headstone still marked with its crafted beauty —encourage quieter moments of reflection. After days of travel and scrutiny, the glimpses merge into a collage of the South; the fragments become whole again.

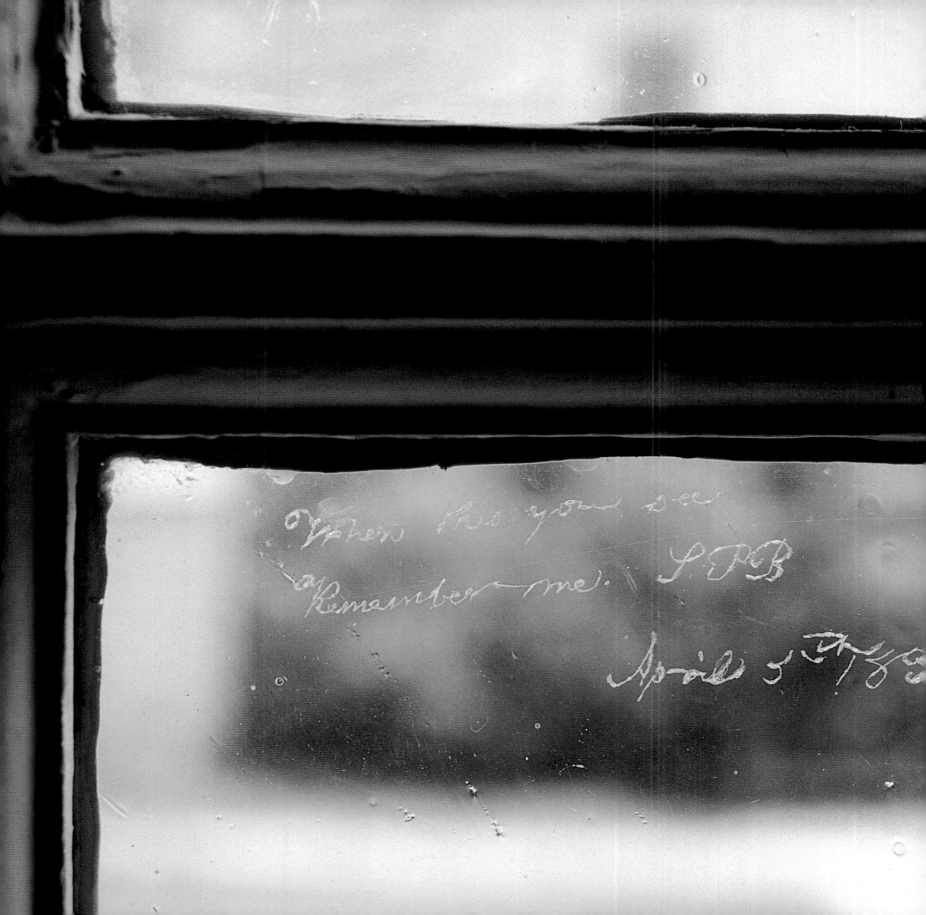

Southerners exult in their gardens, and nowhere more than in the Carolinas is the panoply of gardening styles and tastes so broad. Among the ancestors of the Southern garden are English gardens, both formal and "cottage" style, and Colonial herb gardens, where the ornamental and pragmatic aspects of horticulture meet. Now there are whimsical gardens with teapot posts and flyswatter stepping-stones. There are unruly gardens. And there are gardens laid out with a compass and manicured with scissors. From the "peephole" window of the famed Cupola House in Edenton, the garden is a vision of order, stability, purpose, and hope for the future. Etching her soul in living green, the Southern gardener earns her own immortality.

orches—whether wide sweeping verandahs, screened-in patios off the kitchen, or redwood decks attached to cottages—are an essential feature of Southern living. The kitchen may be the heart of the home, but the porch is its spirit. More than just the threshold to the interior, the porch is an outdoor room for greeting neighbors as they take a stroll, a perch for admiring the garden, and a vantage point for watching children play in the yard. Even the simplest porch has rockers and swings that invite the weary to unwind at the end of the day. Because of its importance to life along the coast, the porch here is never an afterthought; it is often the most dynamic feature of the façade, and much care is taken to dress up its rails, pillars, and columns to make it a welcoming and comfortable place. As social an invention as the porch seems to be, it also has a practical side, sheltering guests as they fold their umbrellas and keeping out the strongest rays of the sun.

There are more than 8,000 miles of coastline in the state of Florida, and they contain an infinite variety of beaches, beach houses, boats, and other diversions. The ocean is everyone's front yard. Outdoor living is a habit of mind and body not just for the young but for the huge retired population as well. Ponce de Leon thought he had failed to locate the Fountain of Youth here, not realizing it was the land itself, with its year-round climate, which has the magical ability to rejuvenate the human spirit.

Almost a wilderness until the early 1900s, Florida still has oases of natural beauty. New communities are pursuing human-scale architecture, and, for those who know where to look, there is even the miracle of a deserted beach.

From thoroughbred stables in the north to the Everglades in the south, Florida is home to a surprisingly varied array of plant and animal life that is often strikingly different even from that of its nearest neighbor, Georgia. With the most exotic climate of any of the continental United States, Florida can be the sort of not-so-civilized terrain where a sinkhole can suddenly reclaim a driveway or an alligator can turn up in the backyard. But for nature lovers and bird watchers it can be the nearest thing to paradise. Even its name calls up visions of tropical enchantment. When Ponce de Leon first sighted the land in April 1513, he called it Florida in honor of the Feast of Flowers. Becoming a state only in 1845, Florida did not experience as profound an involvement with either the Revolution or the Civil War as did the rest of the South. Only recently has Florida truly flowered into the rich and populous state it is today, with no sign of slowing down.

From funky Fernandina Beach at the Georgia state line to Key West, the tourist stops of the tropical paradise of Florida overflow with keepsakes, come-ons, mementos, and doo-dads. As if mimicking the wild tropical colors in nature, builders create spectacles in Florida that can be found nowhere else in the South. It is said, half-seriously, that you need sunglasses on a rainy day to protect yourself from the vacationland atmosphere. With their innate sense of fun, Floridians might turn a spiky shrub into a blooming bush with an old egg carton or trim their porch not just with gingerbread but with gingerbread *men*. There is something utterly charming about Florida's kitsch. Without it, paradise would be too good to be true.

ERIN
BUBBLE SCOUT

If they can send a man to the moon, why can't they send them all?

SSDD (SAME SHIT DIFFERENT DAY)

I'm a stranger here myself

DON'T YELL AT ME I'M A VOLUNTEER!

The Bubble Room

I Love My Mom

Potential Bag Lady

If all the world's a stage I want better...

LIFE'S A BEACH

KISS MY PINK FLAMINGO

SEMI-NATIVE FLORIDIAN

CAN'T KILL THE SPIRIT

Florida

I refuse to have a battle of wits with an unarmed person

If There's A Will, I Want To Be In It.

The Southern
Woman's Garden

Gwen and Ron Griffin, North Carolina

D own a country road from Greensboro on the Piedmont plateau in central North Carolina are the herb shop and gardens of Gwen and Ron Griffin. Both of the Griffins' families have lived in this region for generations. Gwen has a Ph.D. from the University of North Carolina and Ron is an authority on Southern furniture and folk art, but in their gardens, beautiful herbs and flowers convey a relaxing quality of controlled disorder. The sundial in the silver garden keeps time fifteen minutes late, but Ron says the pedestal is too heavy to realign. I like that down-South attitude!

❧

LEFT: *The cast-iron sundial was saved from an antebellum plantation house slated for demolition. Perennial herbs include lamb's ear, rose campion, southernwood, horehound, garlic, chives, and assorted artemisias, wormwoods, mints, and thymes.*
ABOVE: *Hollyhocks are another old-fashioned favorite in today's Southern gardens.*

Gwen's insights into the traditional role of the woman in the rural South are fascinating: "She had to do everything—manage a garden, work in the fields, run a household, and make and repair all the clothes, linens, and other necessities of family life," she observes. "The Southern woman needed to be clever as well as commonsensical to perform all her tasks. And she had to be quite stable, emotionally, to withstand the vicissitudes of daily life in those times."

I always look forward to walking into the workshop where Gwen transforms what she grows into beautiful arrangements, dried bouquets, and wreaths for the home. It reminds me of all those unbelle-like Southern women of the 18th and 19th centuries who accomplished so much with their labor, craftsmanship, and capacity for love.

LEFT: *An early 19th-century weaving chair has been called into service at the table where wreaths are fashioned in Gwen's Weaving Shed.*

ABOVE: *The Weaving Shed, Gwen's studio, is a 19th-century building that was moved onto the property.* **RIGHT:** *All the wreaths, kitchen bunches, and door bunches are assembled from herbs and everlastings grown in the gardens, then hung from rafters or racks to dry cut in the Herb Cottage.* **NEXT PAGES:** *Brick walkways, split-rail fences, hand-painted signs, old clay pots, and weathered furniture rusticate the herb garden in the Carolina way.*

LEMON BALM

An Antebellum
Farmhouse

S u s a n   a n d   P h i l i p   H a r v e y,
N o r t h   C a r o l i n a

The tranquil fishing villages and farming towns along the northeastern coast of North Carolina have changed very little in the last 150 years. For Susan and Philip Harvey, both antiques dealers, their farmhouse on the coast is an ideal spot to settle in with their treasures.

"When we peeked through the front window on the porch, we couldn't believe our eyes," recalls Philip of their first encounter with the dwelling. "The first thing we saw was the marbleized fireplace mantel. As it turned out, most of the original woodwork and painting in the house was intact."

🍂

ABOVE: *An 1830 Federal-style farmhouse received its Southern identity with the addition of a tidy Victorian porch.* FAR LEFT AND LEFT: *Through doors off both sides of the central hall are welcoming twin fireplaces. The interior woodwork remains untouched, revealing many techniques employed to give ordinary pine a high-style look, such as wainscoting painted to resemble mahogany.*

ABOVE: *In the living room, a Queen Anne tea table and country Chippendale chair demonstrate polished skills of 18th-century North Carolina craftsmen.* RIGHT: *An English oil painting hangs over the marbleized mantel.* FAR RIGHT: *The window's abbreviated drapery style is faithful to the period of the house.* BELOW: *Faux finishes are a source of the house's charm.*

Built by the Cullins family in 1830, the house passed in 1860 into the hands of the Bakers, who retained ownership until the Harveys came along. It took Susan and Philip seven years to restore the house, adding such conveniences as plumbing and electricity without sacrificing the home's essential character. Descendants of the Baker family still drop by to admire what they remember as being "the most beautiful woodwork," and can hardly believe it when Philip explains that the mahogany is really painted pine.

Susan is an avid collector of pantry boxes, and Philip has a special interest in handmade decoys, a craft particularly important to this region. "I love the fact that this tradition was more than a hobby in this area," says Philip. "People carved waterfowl decoys to hunt with so they could put food on the table."

Full of wood detailing created to "decoy" observers, the Cullins-Baker house today provides an appropriate roost for Philip's collection.

LEFT: *A still life by an unknown 19th-century North Carolina painter appears to tempt the carved Virginia rooster atop a local hunt board made in 1820. Hand decoration transformed an old English trunk into folk art.*

ABOVE: *There's a place for everything and everybody, including toddlers, in the dining room.* **LEFT**: *Outer Banks shore bird decoys of every feather —beach robins, curlews, and yellowlegs—roost on walls, hearth, and table. The larger-than-life snake is local tree-root folk art.*

North Carolina *197*

LEFT: *The master bedroom features a Connecticut highboy made in 1760 and a Virginia appliqué quilt on the four-poster. The Pilgrim chair at the window is a Centennial reproduction.* ABOVE AND BELOW: *A bedroom is made child-friendly by the addition of a friend's version of* The Peaceable Kingdom, Raggedy Anns *on the old school bench, and expressive rag dolls.*

ABOVE AND BELOW: *A screened-in back porch is the South's original air-conditioned room. For Scott Harvey, it's a place to count heads and tails of his sister Ginger's newest furry friends.*
RIGHT: *The Southern-made hickory furniture of the room was designed to survive bouts of heat and humidity.*

Piedmont Crafts and Cupboards

Charlotte and L.C. Beckerdite, North Carolina

LEFT: *The oak logs of this 1840 house are joined by cement and plaster.* ABOVE: *A locally crafted pine bonnet-top cupboard displays a collection of antique pottery and pewter.*

A lot of people collect things to put in cupboards, but Charlotte Beckerdite collects the cupboards themselves. I first heard about "the cupboard lady," as she is called by friends and admirers, when I started going to the Southern Home Furnishings Market in High Point, North Carolina. Charlotte is the one who got me and my friends interested in antiquing, and I always visit when I go South.

Nowadays, the 1840 log cabin she and her husband, L.C., renovated into their "dream house" is a showplace not only for cupboards, but for quilts, pottery, and antique furniture. "I love the warmth and character in antiques," sums up Charlotte. "They really are like old friends and family to me."

TOP: *In the living room, the Virginia corner cupboard, with original paint, dates from the 1750s.* ABOVE: *The kitchen curtains are made from antique homespun.*

203

ABOVE: *A cannonball bed, named for its post finials, is covered with a 19th-century Pennsylvania quilt. Above it, framed by rare homespun linen show towels made in 1835, a window is dressed with homespun curtains detailed with candlewicking. A miniature Virginia cupboard with glass doors stands on a local scrubbed-top pine table.*

ABOVE: *An expanded loft, furnished with Davidson County rope beds, quilts, and other serviceable antiques, is the dormitory for visiting grandchildren. The dress with pullwork and embroidery on the wall was made long ago by a grandmother for the child who is pictured wearing it in the framed photograph.*

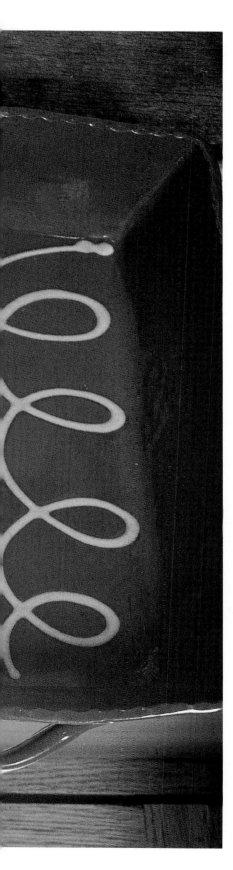

A
Tradition
in Clay

Westmoore Pottery, North Carolina

N o medium speaks more eloquently for our grassroots artistic heritage than Carolina clay," wrote folk pottery authority John A. Burrison in a 1985 essay.

Mary and David Farrell are young potters working in the centuries-old traditions of the folk potters of the North Carolina Piedmont, a region blessed with natural deposits of high-quality clays. The Farrells not only built their Westmoore Pottery kiln in Seagrove; they put up the building themselves and live behind the store. There, they fashion faithful reproductions of the stoneware first made and used in the area in the 18th and 19th centuries.

The history-minded couple's special interests are the Moravian styles created by potters of the German immigrant sect that settled in Forsyth County in the 1750s. Distinguished by vivid colors and patterns, the pottery preserves a Central European heritage that found a new home in our South.

ABOVE: *Moravian reproductions include plates, mugs, ramekins, sugar jars, pitchers, and preserves pots.*

ABOVE AND RIGHT: *From mixing the clay with water and shaping it on the wheel, to adding decoration, drying, and firing, a month's time is required to complete a single piece.* LEFT: *A freehand design applied by "slip trailing" adorns two redware bakers.*

Backwoods Blacksmith

Jerry Darnell, North Carolina

S mell that?" asks Jerry Darnell with an enthusiastic sniff. "That's the sweet smell of Pocahontas forging coal!" Darnell, a high school physics teacher, has devoted his free time over the past twenty years to mastering blacksmithing.

Working at a forge where temperatures reach 2,300 degrees Fahrenheit, Darnell fashions stubborn iron into everything from simple nails, latches, and hinges to ornate gate pieces and chandeliers.

"There is a strong tradition of craftsmanship in my family," explains Jerry. "My father was a welder and my great-great-grandfather, David Kennedy, was one of the best-known gunsmiths in the Carolinas."

🌿

LEFT: *A working blacksmith's shop is equipped with 18th- and 19th-century tools collected from local flea markets and antique shops.* RIGHT: *At his Mill Creek Forge, Jerry Darnell produces hardware for decorative and practical needs.*

Low Country
Treasure

Middleton Place, South Carolina

LEFT AND ABOVE: *A curvilinear barn gable echoes the façade of the main house. The original plantation occupied 10,000 acres with terraced gardens and rice fields leading down to the Ashley River.*

Twelve miles upstream from Charleston, on the Ashley River, stands the gloriously restored plantation of Middleton Place. Devoted to preserving the agricultural traditions of the Low Country and interpreting the lives of ten generations of a powerful and accomplished South Carolina family, Middleton Place is one of the South's greatest historical treasures.

Much of the credit for Middleton's resurrection belongs to Charles Duell, who inherited the property in 1969—acreage that has remained in the same family since the 1690s! He resisted advice to sell off his ancestral lands even though, at the time, the gardens and most of the buildings were in ruins.

"It sounds corny," he says, "but I have a strong sense of history, which I think is essential to our psyche, to a happy way of life, because it provides a continuum instead of a vacuum."

TOP: *Middleton Place House is the surviving wing of the original Georgian residence, burned in 1865 by Union troops and further damaged in 1886.*
ABOVE: *Today's re-creation of plantation life features livestock.*

211

ABOVE: *Portraits of four generations of Middletons, who lived in the house from 1741 until the Civil War, along with some of the family silver, are on display in the main room.*

RIGHT: *Both the silver epergne and Neoclassical architectural candlesticks were acquired by an early Middleton on a trip to London in 1771.*

ABOVE: *Empire furniture made in Philadelphia, about 1815, occupies the music room. The paintings are copies of favorite works in European galleries brought to Charleston by the family 150 years ago. The French repoussé tiara on the table was worn by Mary Middleton when she attended court during her husband's service as minister to Russia.*

ABOVE: *The stifling summer heat in the Low Country dictated that heavy winter hangings be replaced with mosquito netting and light dimity.* **RIGHT**: *Made in Charleston in the early 19th century, the bed features footposts carved with a rice motif to honor the regional cash crop.* **BELOW**: *The child's room, with its study desk and array of Early American toys, reflects the interests of the privileged children of the day.*

In attempting to re-create
the self-contained, self-sustaining
economic unit of the Southern
plantation, Middleton rebuilt its
barns, workshops, and livestock pens and recruited craftspeople and farm workers
from the area to oversee the
routines of daily life.

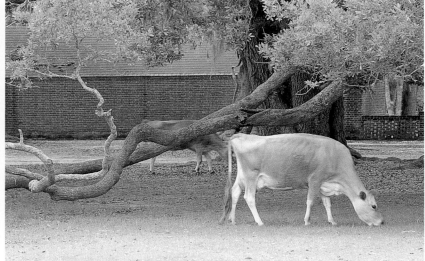

Today, Middleton buzzes with activity. There are beautiful 18th-century French formal gardens, cultivated rice fields, a breathtaking allée of camellias, one hillside planted with nearly 60,000 azaleas, and living exhibits of dozens of the practical arts of early farm and domestic life.

Duell went to great lengths to locate equipment and elements authentic to the rice and cotton plantations of the era. Searching on the estate itself, buying at auctions, and borrowing from regional museums, he acquired old plows and flails, hand tools of carpenters, blacksmiths, and other artisans, carriages, and the cypress dugout canoes paddled through rice fields and marshes.

Even livestock had to pass the litmus test of authenticity. The cattle grazing in the pastures here are either Jerseys or short-legged Devons, the first breed imported from England.

Everything about Middleton is authentic. Even in its fragrant, deliciously Southern 18th-century rose garden, no modern hybrids are allowed. As one staff member says, "We're not trying to play Scarlett O'Hara here."

LEFT: *Martha Deweese, a Middleton Place staff member, tends goats in a livestock "exhibit."*

A Planter's World

Walnut Grove, South Carolina

Walnut Grove may not look like a Tara, but when Charles Moore, a pioneer of means, established his farm home on the western frontier of South Carolina in 1758, he gave it all the ingredients of a plantation. Today, restored as a museum home open to the public, it offers a fascinating glimpse into the self-contained world of the Southern planter. Small outbuildings include a wheat house, meat house, root cellar, well house, blacksmith house, and various barns. A one-room schoolhouse provided Moore's children with a gentleman's knowledge of Latin and Greek, and an herb garden yielded medicines, flavorings, cosmetics, and other useful household products.

A visit here reveals not only the complex array of skills required to operate a back-country plantation, but also the vision, vigor, and courage required to embark on an enterprise most of us would consider daunting today.

❧

ABOVE: *Built in the South Carolina wilderness 230 years ago, this dwelling is a rural variant on sophisticated Georgian homes of the coast.* LEFT: *A mule barn, a blacksmith's shop, and a well house are typically primitive outbuildings.* BELOW: *Education began at home in the log schoolhouse Moore built for his children and those of neighboring planters.*

221

FAR LEFT: *A sleeping loft in the kitchen suggests it served as quarters for the original owners until the main house was ready.* LEFT: *Household items included a corn-shuck broom and a cradle equipped with exercise bar and "sugar teat," an early version of the pacifier.*

ABOVE: *A kitchen a few steps behind the main house reduced the danger of fire and spared the family, if not the servants, from the additional heat during the torrid Southern summer.*

ABOVE FAR LEFT: *In the dining room, the pine breakfront, made in Greenville, is overlaid with mahogany, an exotic and expensive wood rarely found in frontier homes.* ABOVE LEFT: *By tilting platters forward in the rack, the Early American housewife saved herself unnecessary dusting.* BELOW LEFT: *The large dormitory room upstairs had many other uses besides sleeping.* RIGHT: *The "heavenly blue" of bed and chest was a favorite color of the Colonial period.*

ABOVE: *In the master bedroom, a display of a sword and splint-lock pistols pays homage to Kate Moore Barry, a Southern female counterpart of Paul Revere, who once took to her horse to round up local forces during the Revolutionary War.*

ABOVE: *The plantation-made Hepplewhite pine bed has posts carved in Charleston and a linsey-woolsey coverlet with a double fringe. Map over dressing table was brought to America by Charles Moore from his native Ireland.*

New South Sophistication

Nancy and James Braithwaite, Georgia

Atlanta is the capital of the New South and the gateway for Southerners bound for New York, London, Europe, and the rest of the world. Not surprisingly, many of its homes reflect a sophisticated outlook but keep touch with their precious Southern heritage. Nancy and James Braithwaite's home is a good example. The Braithwaites have taken their suburban ranch house and given it a personality that is as up to date as Atlanta and as traditional as Dixie.

"We live in a disposable culture," Nancy says, explaining why she has collected so many beautiful old objects from the region. "Antiques are objects that have endured. They give you a sense of permanence."

Her eye for antiques is matched by her ability to mix them effectively with new pieces. "I don't necessarily like things that are trendy, but I think mixing the new with the old can bring nice surprises to a home," and that's exactly what she's done in her house. Her approach to decorating is simply to edit out what doesn't work. This ongoing practice of collecting and using only things that have real meaning to her gives Nancy's home a true integrity.

❧

ABOVE: *A 1950s ranch house bears a redesigned façade.* LEFT: *Black-on-white scheme accents folk art and antique wooden furniture in the living room.*

ABOVE: *Traffic in the family room dictated the choice of durable new wicker, but the rare black Amish coverlet (circa 1800) on the wall, draped with a pillow cover for color, sets the tone.* **RIGHT**: *In the hall are a board-top English bench and a 19th-century duck decoy carved in flight.*

LEFT: *"Simplicity without intimidation" is the owner's motto, as demonstrated by this burled ash bowl on a walnut beaded board table from the 1820s.* **RIGHT**: *An elegant 1830s demilune table made of Southern pine is framed by steel French park chairs.*

ABOVE: *New tiles and old hunt board perpetuate the black-and-white theme in the modern kitchen, while another old hunt board stands in traditional counterpoint. The pen-and-ink sketch is by Southern artist Benny Andrews.* **LEFT**: *A screened-in porch, converted into a congenial dining room, opens onto patio and garden. Against the wall, the hunt table of yellow pine from 1800 has starred in a Georgia "neat pieces" furniture exhibition organized by Nancy. The paintings are by Bill Trayler, a folk artist who worked in Alabama in the 1940s.*

ABOVE: *Roman blinds let in enough sun to illuminate a 20th-century iron bed, its finials and trim embossed with gold, purchased in Rome. A North Carolina swan and Moravian blanket chest provide the Southern accent.*

ABOVE: *In the bedroom, a 19th-century walnut table is accompanied by a suede-seated bamboo chair and a child's chair, made of oak around 1900, presented to the owners as a gift on the birth of their daughter.* RIGHT: *Baskets of rolled towels, a bouquet of daisies, and white paneled walls give a fresh look to the bathroom.*

Plantation Plain

Bettye and John Wagner, Georgia

Over the years, I've noticed that people who collect antiques become more aware of our history and more sensitive to the traditional arts and crafts of their region of the country.

One such couple is Bettye and John Wagner, who first became intrigued with antiquing upon visiting Williamsburg, Virginia, and Old Salem, North Carolina. "Something clicked on my trips there," Bettye recalls. "It totally changed my life and life-style, by making me aware of our heritage."

Since then, she has avidly searched for authentic Southern antiques and folk pieces. I especially admire the painted wood furniture she has discovered and brought into her home. Although newly built, the farmhouse-style dwelling follows a Georgia floor plan dating from 1840, called "Plantation

LEFT: *The breakfast nook leading to the breezeway is filled with a mix of Georgia "neat pieces," including a stripped pine jelly cupboard from the 1850s.* ABOVE: *A wishing well and a split-rail fence countrify the yard.*

TOP: *A Plantation Plain floor plan from 1840 gives a new suburban dwelling the intimate space of an old country farmhouse.* ABOVE: *The herb garden has such traditional pieces as a sundial, bee skep, and a terra-cotta hare.*

ABOVE: *Authentic colors of the South are preserved on such rare painted pieces as the red pewter cupboard from north Georgia in the dining/family room.* **LEFT**: *The dining room has an early Georgia-made two-drawer slab, a distinctly Southern piece, later termed a hunt board.*

Plain," complete with an old-style front porch, "perfect for long, hot summer days in the South," Bettye notes.

Inside, the couple left floors unfinished, added exposed beams to the ceilings, and covered new walls with paint amended with flour to imitate whitewash for an aged look. The rooms are a wonderful backdrop for the ever-changing specimens from the couple's collections. Bettye has a knack for creating charming vignettes, both in the house and out in the garden. A whimsical homespun doll or one of the carved, stuffed, or clay animals in her country menagerie may brighten a somber corner or a straight-backed chair. With these amusing grace notes, Bettye combines her newfound love of history with her ongoing joy of life.

RIGHT: *The vivid mustard-yellow cupboard made in about 1850 in west Georgia, in the kitchen.*

ABOVE: *In a youth's bedroom, calico garments, rag dolls, and an antique infant's bed are reminders of an 18th-century childhood.*
LEFT: *In the master bedroom, the four-poster bed—built from heart of pine by a local craftsman—comes complete with a favorite costume for the South, the canopy. The linsey-woolsey coverlet has a pinecone and snowflake woven pattern. The 1760 Chippendale dresser came from New York State.*

A Feast of Oysters

Pat and Rip
Benton, Georgia

Nothing expresses the hospitality of the South better than an all-you-can-eat Low Country oyster roast. Formality is put aside as tables are covered with newspapers instead of starched linens, then heaped with piles of the freshest fare of the nearby coastal waters and surrounding farm fields. So I couldn't resist when Pat and Rip Benton of Blanche's Courtyard Restaurant on Saint Simons Island invited me to go elbow to elbow for an unforgettable feast.

ABOVE LEFT, BELOW LEFT, AND ABOVE: *Oysters are roasted over an open fire, with plenty of wet burlap bags to keep them from drying out.* **RIGHT:** *A hungry crowd digs in to a feast served buffet style.*

Pat Benton's Oyster Roast

Pat's fare might include crawfish, blue crabs, boiled shrimp, barbecued ribs, corn on the cob, cole slaw, hush puppies, and, of course, oysters. As Pat says, "Eat, drink, and be messy!"

Shovel

½ of a 55-gallon drum or a piece of roofing tin, fitted with wire handles

Enough charcoal and wood for a strong fire

8–12 oysters per person (depending on the rest of the meal)

Lots of water-soaked burlap bags

Dig a hole big enough to accommodate the drum. Fill it with a mixture of charcoal and wood and get the fire going. Extra wood will keep the flame hot for the 20 to 40 minutes necessary to roast the oysters.

If the oysters are in clusters, separate them. Scrub the oysters thoroughly, then spread them in two layers on the bottom of the drum or tin. Cover the oysters with the wet burlap sacks.

Lower the drum or tin into the fire. As the burlap sacks dry out, pull them off and soak them again. From time to time, use a shovel to stir the oysters so that they steam evenly.

When the shells of three-quarters of the oysters have opened, remove them all from the container. Spread the table with old newspapers, pass out the garden gloves and oyster knives, and dig in.

serves a crowd

Hush Puppies

The hush puppy purportedly got
its name because it was tossed to
howling dogs to keep them quiet,
but people have also begged for
this time-honored Southern treat
since its invention.

      2 cups yellow cornmeal
     ½ cup all-purpose flour
    2½ teaspoons baking powder
    1½ teaspoons salt
      1 tablespoon sugar
     ¾ cup milk
      2 eggs, well beaten
     ¼ cup chopped pimientos (for
        color)
      1 tablespoon chopped jalapeño
        peppers
     ¼ cup chopped onions
        Vegetable oil for deep-frying

In a large bowl, combine all ingredients except oil, blending
well to remove all lumps. Batter
should be stiff. Heat oil in a
deep pot until very hot but not
smoking. Drop rounded tea-
spoonfuls of batter into hot fat
and fry until golden brown.
Hush puppies should float
when done.

MAKES ABOUT **36**

FAR LEFT: *Scenes from
the Bentons' oyster roast show the
prying tools, bandannas
for napkins/bibs, the newspaper-
covered buffet table, and
the succulent crabs.* LEFT:
*After the oysters come a
variety of Southern specialties,
including crawfish, a
delicacy often steamed and
served with hot sauce.*

An Inventor's
Tropical Paradise

The Thomas A. Edison Home,
Florida

T homas A. Edison, the electrician, is visiting here," announced the *Fort Myers Press* in a single line in 1885, reporting with remarkable restraint the most important event in the town's history.

Edison had come to Florida on doctor's orders and promptly chose the bamboo-lined banks of the Caloosahatchee River for his winter home. The home and the breezeway-connected guest house that he personally designed for the location were some of the original prefabricated buildings in America. Built in sections in Fairfield, Maine, the structures were shipped in four schooners to Fort Myers and assembled on the grounds in 1886.

In moving to Florida long before that state was served by rail (not to mention air), Edison was something of a pioneer

❧

ABOVE AND LEFT: *A prefab structure built in Maine, Edison's house combines New England Victorian traditions and tropical necessities—porches with French doors and wicker lounge furniture.*

snowbird. He built his own resort, complete with swimming pool, many decades before the idea became the model for Florida living.

One professional reason Edison was happy to spend winters in the South was that the tropical climate gave this zealous experimental gardener a chance to tinker with plants.

Using every open space, he established more than 600 rare and beautiful species that have flourished into a botanical fantasy. For Edison, no plant was too bizarre.

Although his rubber experiments in Florida never yielded the commercial success of so many of his other discoveries, his Seminole Lodge remains a testament to Thomas Edison's genius and his innumerable contributions to modern life.

ABOVE FAR LEFT: *Edison is flanked by industrialist cronies Henry Ford and Harvey Firestone in a picture preserved in his Florida office.* ABOVE LEFT AND BELOW FAR LEFT: *The labs at Seminole Lodge were devoted mostly to cement research* LEFT AND RIGHT: *Using his patented Portland cement, Edison built one of the area's first modern swimming pools in 1900, an innovation soon common throughout the South.*

LEFT AND BELOW: Edison grew trees and shrubs potentially useful to industry for their products and byproducts.

LEFT: *The second Mrs. Edison erected her birdhouses on stilts over the water to foil her predatory cats.*

A Southern Original

Evelyn **F**. **B**artlett,
Bonnet **H**ouse,
Florida

J ust over a sand dune from a jumbled collection of beach-front hotels, restaurants, and condominiums in Fort Lauderdale lies the 35-acre estate of Bonnet House, once described as "a stunning testament to another time and to a witty, idiosyncratic vision."

I love wandering through this Caribbean–plantation-style house, built during the 1920s, with its spacious verandah and open courtyard plan. It is full of unexpected sights and charming juxtapositions, all thanks to the worldly and whimsical tastes of the couple who designed and decorated it. Frederic and Evelyn F. Bartlett were accomplished post-Impressionist painters, as well as collectors of antiques and curios from all parts of the world. Today their home and collections are open to visitors under the aegis of the Florida Trust, and Evelyn Bartlett has continued to spend several months a year in the house since her husband's death in 1953.

An outstanding example of an eccentric (but to me fascinating) living style, the Bonnet House is important because it pre-

ABOVE: Swans, along with herons, egrets, native manatee, and rare monkeys, inhabit groves and waterways. RIGHT AND FAR RIGHT: Bonnet House is a testament to the wit of its builder, who placed cast-concrete fish at its entrances.

serves some of the visual and environmental heritage of our southeastern coast. Elements of this country's European roots are contained here, but the buildings and grounds are unmistakably in the Florida vernacular tradition.

Only Florida materials were used to build the house, with masonry blocks formed and poured on the site for walls, and local cypress cut for the shingles and panels. Decorative elements, both painted and sculpted, also echo the colorful flora and fauna of the tropics. Even the name of the house comes from a plant indigenous to the surrounding sloughs, the Bonnet lily.

The flair, good humor, and wide-open spirit that created Bonnet House reflect America's artistic energy in the 1920s. Today it survives as one of the outstanding house museums of the South. Its exotic and expensive way of life may not be easy to duplicate, but it is a rich source of inspiration for our own homes.

LEFT: *The subtropical world of southern Florida is called to mind in the vivid colors applied to the verandah's doors, windows, gates, and doorways.* RIGHT: *A ceiling mural by Frederic Bartlett on the verandah depicts the local creatures of the sea. Evelyn Bartlett, also an artist, painted the fishnet.*

LEFT AND RIGHT: *The call of the wild is playfully reflected in the colorful menagerie of carved carousel figures and temple animals from the Far East that peek out from doorways, alcoves, and other perches along the verandah. The artist's own tongue-in-cheek portraits of animals and historical figures also hang here. A spiral staircase leads through painted fronds to an observation tower.*

FAR LEFT: *The shell room owes its existence to a lifetime of beachcombing. After elaborate borders and other patterns were painted on the walls, shells were set in wet concrete.*
ABOVE AND LEFT: *Cypress paneling in the dining room shows off the catch of the day—an exhibit of mounted tropical fish, always in pairs.*
RIGHT: *Another collection with a seashell theme is on view in the scallop-framed cupboard.*

LEFT: *In the deliberate disharmony of the studio, the artist's work is set against the raw beauty of an exposed concrete block wall.*
ABOVE AND BELOW: *The drawing room evokes the Caribbean with seashell-shaped chairs and Cuban floor tiles. The columns at the doorways were reclaimed from an old Spanish church.*

ABOVE: *The eye-fooling floor, painted to resemble marble, is an example of Bartlett's lighthearted use of his artistic talents in embellishing the home.* LEFT: *The bust of a veiled woman, the tour de force of an unknown Victorian sculptor, shares the elaborately carved marble mantel with seashell keepsakes made by sailors for distant loved ones.*

LEFT: *Under the spreading ficus tree, potted orchids reflect Evelyn Bartlett's lifelong gardening obsession.* RIGHT: *A thatched-roof "chickee" spanning the pond was rebuilt by Seminole Indians using materials and techniques traditional to the Florida tribe.* BELOW RIGHT AND BOTTOM RIGHT: *Large sculpted pieces with a classical lineage make effective garden ornaments amid the lush tropical vegetation of the grounds.*

A Romantic Cottage
on Love Lane

Mary Emmerling, Florida

The South turns to two great bodies of water for its nour-
ishment and inspiration, the Atlantic Ocean and the Gulf
of Mexico, and Florida enjoys the best of both. This village with
its elaborate Victorian and native Conch houses has the friendly
atmosphere of a small Southern town transplanted to the beach.
A day's worth of errands to the fish store, market, and café
always yields a week's worth of gossip. Key West's artistic and
crafts traditions make it even more stimulating.

"Going down to sunset" is an end-of-day ritual here. Tourists
and locals alike saunter down to the beach to meet, chat, and

❧

ABOVE: *From behind the lacy porch balusters on her
hundred-year-old Key West cottage, Mary finds it easy to adopt the
it-can-wait-until-mañana attitude.* LEFT AND BELOW: *Mary's
signature hearts and Southern magnolias set the scene for
relaxed entertaining on the deck.*

Chris Mead

267

gaze in awe at the spectacular sight of the sun sinking into Gulf waters. The event always elicits a round of applause and sometimes a rousing ovation. There are jugglers, clowns, musicians, and food vendors, and it's usually hard to get the kids back to our cottage on Love Lane for supper.

Sometimes Key West strikes me as a Southern turquoise version of the Hamptons on Long Island. The relaxed, un-hurried pace of life, the cour-tesy and talkativeness of the natives, and the impulse to so-cialize outdoors all make for a congenial *mañana* life-style. When I come to Key West, the southernmost town in the continental United States, I feel I'm coming home.

LEFT AND RIGHT: *In the living room, an old painted kitchen table, cut down to size, displays Mary's ever-changing collec-tion of shells gathered from walks along the Florida coastline. Framed botanical prints and the vintage fabric used for pillows both evoke the flora of the South. Antique lace tablecloths take on new life as effective window curtains.*

Chris Mead

LEFT: *Fresh gladioli provide a tropical note on the dining room's buffet/bar—a sorting table from Texas. Tile floors throughout the house are ideal for sandy feet.*

LEFT: *The turn-top table, or lazy Susan, an Early American solution for self-service dining, comes in handy today.*
RIGHT: *Wooden kitchen shelves and newly installed French doors to the deck are typical of Mary's open decorating style.*

ABOVE: *Mary's twig heart bed is fittingly dressed with Country Basket sheets of her own design. A painting of a beach house by the Key West artist Donna Hayes provides a touch of local color. Shutters are a tried-and-true Southern convention for creating privacy without losing balmy breezes.*

ABOVE: *Hues of the coral reef are captured in the bedroom's old prints, a turquoise country cupboard, and hibiscus and bougainvillea blooms.* RIGHT: *Vases, made in Key West by Whitehead Street Pottery, are part of a collection Mary uses throughout the house.* BELOW: *New white pine matches the original cottage walls, milled from Dade County timber at the turn of the century.*

ABOVE AND LEFT: *The intense colors and forms of the tropics create a dramatic stage for entertaining by night. Subtle lighting calls attention to the lush plant life, while hurricane lamps give an aura of romance to the supper table.*

Chris Mead

Directory of Stores, Galleries, and Craftsmen

Alabama

Blackburn-Mastich House
Route 5, Box 84
Athens 35611
(205) 233-4143
Southern furniture and accessories displayed in room settings. Specializes in handmade hooked, braided, and rag rugs. Call for appointment.

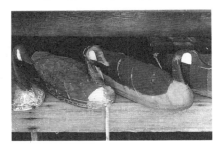

Mary Elizabeth's Quilts and Crafts
332 Fairhope Avenue
Fairhope 36532
(205) 928-4633
Custom-order quilts, restorations, and advice on care. Also carries fabrics, quilt patterns, and books on quilting.

Robert Cargo Folk Art Gallery
2314 6th Street
Tuscaloosa 35401
(205) 753-8884
In New York area:
(201) 322-8732
Contemporary Alabama folk arts, paintings, sculpture, walking canes, painted gourds, 20th-century Afro-American quilts, plain-style furniture of 19th-century Alabama, alkaline-glazed Alabama stoneware, and face jugs.

Florida

Antique 'n' Country
1965 Aloma Avenue
Winter Park 32792
(408) 657-1863
Antiques and collectibles, as well as country decorating items.

Calico Cat
5101 East Busch Boulevard
Tampa 33617
(813) 988-0481
Country home furnishings and accessories, folk art, quilts, baskets, and brass.

Cobblestone Alley Antiques
639 North Citrus Avenue
Crystal River 32629
(904) 795-0060
Contemporary folk art, accessories, and herbs.

Fast Buck Freddie's
500 Duval Street
Key West 33040
(305) 294-2007
A specialty department store featuring lighthearted table-top accessories and giftware.

Fletcher on Duval
1024 Duval Street
Key West 33040
(305) 294-2032
Design and sales of fossilized coral, Keystone furniture, and architectural elements, along with mountain laurel table and console bases.

Gulfglade Orchids, Inc.
7801 North Airport Road
Naples 33942
(813) 597-3936
Growers and hybridizers of orchids, with a wide variety of genera from seedlings to mature plants. Mail order.

Indian Lane Farm Antiques
2317 Segovia Avenue
Jacksonville 32217
(904) 733-3169
American furniture, folk art, and textiles from the 17th through the 19th century.

Lamp Post Antiques, Inc.
3955 Riverside Avenue
Jacksonville 32205
(904) 388-3513
English and American country furniture in cherry, walnut, and pine.

Memories Antiques and Country
6521 Orange Drive
Davie 33314
(305) 581-2490
Antique oak furniture and collectibles.

Norma M. Renner
30 Hilton Haven Drive
Key West 33040
(305) 296-3373
Woodcarvings and paintings of country scenes by Norma Renner.

Oakhurst Antiques, Inc.
7743 Old Oakhurst Road
Seminole 34646
(813) 398-6880

Specializing in country furniture and accessories in original paints and finishes.

The Posh Pineapple
560 Indian Rocks Road
Belleair Bluffs 33540
(813) 586-3006
Country furnishings and collectibles.

Top of the Hill Antique Mall, Inc.
7979 131 Street North
Seminole 34646
(813) 399-2449; 397-4477
American country antiques, quilts, folk art, and herbs.

Whitehead Street Pottery
1011 Whitehead Street
Key West 33040
(305) 294-5067
A studio specializing in stoneware, porcelain, and raku-fired vessels. Mail order.

Wisteria Corner Antique Mall
225 North Main
P.O. Box 741
High Springs 32643
(904) 454-3555; 454-3885
American and European antiques, collectibles, and handcrafted items. Mail order.

Georgia

American Folk Heritage
Route 2, Box 852
Hull 30646
(404) 548-7034
American country furniture from the 18th and 19th centuries. Early quilts and rugs, as well as folk art and accessories.

The Antique Store of Marietta
113 Church Street
Marietta 30060
(404) 428-3376
American country antiques and decorating services.

Barbara Palmer Antiques
417 East Bay Street
Savannah 31401
(912) 238-0200
18th- and 19th-century furniture and accessories; primitive, country, and period pieces.

Betty's Prim-A-Tiques
Mountain Mercantile
115 Church Street
Marietta 30064
(404) 421-5250
Custom-crafted willow furniture and accessories.

Bob and Julia Christian
  Decorative Art
415 Abercorn Street
Savannah 31401
(404) 234-6866
Specializing in custom-painted faux finishes. Decorative items available.

Deanne Levison American
  Antiques
2995 Lookout Place NE
Atlanta 30305
(404) 264-0106
American country furniture from the 18th and 19th centuries. Accessories and collectibles.

Francis McNairy Antiques
411 Abercorn Street
Savannah 31401
(912) 232-6411
American and English antiques, decorative accessories, and American furniture from the 19th century.

The Heritage Collection
The Village at Roswell Summit
1085 Holcomb Bridge Road
Roswell 30076
(404) 642-6272
Early American country antiques, furnishings, and accessories.

James Kirkland Ltd.
12 West Harris Street
Savannah 31401
(912) 238-3902
Antique and reproduction garden ornaments and furniture. Mail order.

Jim Lord American Antiques
855 Grimes Bridge Road
Roswell 30075
(404) 642-9958
American country antiques, quilts, and folk art, with a special emphasis on Southern pieces.

Little Street Gallery
20 Little Street
Commerce 30529
(404) 335-3356
Southern folk and decorative arts, alkaline-glazed pottery, furniture, and fine arts. Mail order.

Mulberry House
1028 Canton Street
Roswell 30188
(404) 998-6851
Specializing in country furniture and accessories. Also fine English and oriental porcelain.

The Tabby House
105 Retreat
Saint Simons Island 31522
(912) 638-2257
English antiques and Low Country furnishings.

Kentucky

The Breckinridge Gallery, Inc.
201 South Broadway
Georgetown 40511
(502) 863-3163
Fine furniture, silver, brass, and cut glass.

Clifton Anderson
112 West 4th Street
Lexington 40508
(606) 255-7108
Regional art and antiques of the early 19th century.

Dianne R. Mink
108 Ashlock Street
Lancaster 40444
(606) 792-4983
Country antiques, textiles, folk art, and formal country furniture. Mail order.

Jarvis Heights Antiques
3277 Cynthia Road
Georgetown 40324
(502) 863-2356
Period and country furniture refinished or as is.

Jo and Travis Rawlings
311 and 400 South Winter Street
Midway 40347
(606) 846-4550
Regional furniture, brass, and accessories from the early 18th to the early 19th century.

John Randolph Farmer
920 West Main Street
P.O. Box 537
Princeton 42445
(502) 365-6376
*18th- and 19th-century arts
and antiques.*

JWE & Co.
226 Holiday Manor Walk
Louisville 40222
(502) 426-5643
*Redware, antique quilts, contempo-
rary folk art, and custom-made
furniture.*

Karen Graves Antiques
110 Central Avenue
Pewee Valley 40056
(502) 241-6308
*American furniture, folk art, light-
ing, and paintings of the early 19th
century.*

Loch Lea Antiques
410 Main Street
P.O. Box 31
Paris 40361
(609) 987-4604
*Early 19th-century furniture, quilts,
and furnishings.*

Ruth C. Scully American Country
  Antiques
5237 Bardstown Road
Louisville 40291
(502) 491-9501
*Early 19th-century American coun-
try furniture, decorative arts, textiles, baskets, and folk art.*

Shelly Zegart Quilts, Etc.
122 River Road
Louisville 40207
(502) 897-3819
*Antique quilts, exhibits, and ap-
praisals. Video mail-order catalog
available.*

Wallin Forge
Route 1, Box 65
Sparta 41086
(606) 567-7201
*Custom-made hand-forged iron-
work in original designs.*

Yesterday Antiques
P.O. Box 135
Burgin 40310
(606) 748-5588
*Country and primitive furniture
and accessories.*

Zee Faulkner Antiques
113 Walton at East Main Street
Lexington 40508
(606) 252-1309
*English and Dutch furniture and
accessories, specializing in Dutch
brass, Staffordshire, and unusual
accessories.*

Louisiana

Architectural Accents
1025 Marshall Street
Shreveport 71101
(318) 425-5260
*Vintage and reproduction architec-
tural details.*

Bobby and Katy Johnson
508 Cedar Street
P.O. Box 274
Westlake 70669
(318) 433-3156
*Country antiques, specializing in
handmade tin lighting fixtures.*

Lucullus, Culinary Antiques
610 Chartres Street
New Orleans 70130
(504) 528-9620
*English and Continental furniture;
porcelain, silver, and ironwork re-
lating to eating, drinking, or cooking from the 17th to the 19th
century.*

Meyerhouse Antiques
1517 Diane Drive
Sulphur 70663
(318) 625-5187
*American country folk art, painted
furniture, and accessories.*

Serendipity Antiques
507 East Main Street
New Roads 70760
(504) 638-4369
*American country antiques and ac-
cessories.*

Toni Perkin's Clementine's
  Antiques
Route 1, Box 50A
New Roads 70760
(504) 638-7284
*American country antiques
and wicker.*

Maryland

Aleida V. Snell's Americana
  Unlimited
15716 Bondy Lane
Gaithersburg 20878
(301) 926-1727
Decorative painter and folk artist.

All of Us Americans Folk Art
Box 5943
Bethesda 20814
(301) 652-4626
*Southern antique furniture, wood
figures, quilts, and paintings. Mail
order.*

Americana Marketplace
8118 Woodmont Avenue
Bethesda 20814
(301) 652-9473
*Period and country antiques, folk
art, and accessories.*

Cathy Smith Antique Quilts
P.O. Box 681
Severna Park 21146
(301) 647-3503
*Antique quilts from mid-19th to
early 20th century.*

Charles S. Riser
Route 1, Box 380
Boonsboro 21713
(301) 432-6629
*Antique Southern baskets, stone-
ware, textiles, decoys, and dolls.
Mail order.*

Don and June Risser Country
Antiques
104 Spring Valley Heights Drive
Hagerstown 21740
(301) 790-1245
*Nineteenth-century primitive coun-
try furniture and accessories.*

Douglas Cramer Antiques
Route 1, Box 175D
Hagerstown 21740
(301) 739-0525
*Country furniture, folk art, and
textiles.*

James Cramer and Dean Johnson
Route 1, Box 28A
Keedysville 21756
(301) 432-6574
*Southern fabric folk dolls, hand-
made, numbered, and signed.*

John C. Newcomer and Assoc.
32 West Baltimore Street
P.O. Box 130
Funkstown 21734
(301) 790-1327
*American antiques, folk art, quilts,
and accessories.*

Lewis and Clark Antiques
Beaver Creek Antique Market
Hagerstown 21740
(301) 739-8075
*Country furniture, quilts,
and accessories.*

Noah's Ark
2909 Old Ocean City Road
P.O. Box 1050
Salisbury 21801
(301) 546-9522
*Original design folk art wood carv-
ings. Mail order.*

Pieces of Old
P.O. Box 65130
Baltimore 21209
(301) 366-4949
*Victorian accessories and vintage
fabrics. Mail order.*

Stella Rubin
12300 Glen Road
Potomac 20854
(301) 948-4187
*Antique quilts from early 19th
to early 20th century. Baskets,
country furniture, and decorative
objects.*

Trela Antiques
2950 Baldwin Mill Road
Baldwin 21013
(301) 557-9827
*American country and formal fur-
niture and accessories from the
18th and early 19th centuries.*

Mississippi

Dressing Up at Bobbie King's
667 Dulling Avenue
Woodland Hills Shopping Center
Jackson 39216
(601) 362-9803
*Antique and contemporary bed lin-
ens, jewelry, and accessories.*

Fridge's
838-R Lakeland Drive
Jackson 39216
(601) 366-8459
*Antique furniture, collectibles, and
tableware.*

Martha Flannigan's Antiques
P.O. Box 8733
Jackson 39204
(601) 878-6684
Southern antique furniture.

Shearwater Potter, Ltd.
P.O. Box 737
102 Shearwater Drive
Ocean Springs 39564
(601) 875-7320
*Pottery by James Anderson and the
late Peter Anderson.*

William's Antiques
Route 2, Box 431
Oxford 38655
(601) 234-5171
*Primitive and country furniture and
accessories. Restoration of antiques.
Mail order.*

North
Carolina

Crawford's Antiques "On the
Village Green"
Route 9, Box 240C
Goldsboro 27530
(919) 778-4126
*Oriental rugs, silver, ceramics, and
fine furniture.*

Griffin's
5109 Vickrey Chapel Road
Greensboro 27407
(919) 454-3362
*Southern antiques, furniture, de-
coys, textiles, baskets, and other
folk art. Mail order.*

Mill Creek Forge and
Blacksmith Shop
Route 2, Box 494B
Seagrove 28341
(919) 464-3888
(919) 692-6914
*A traditional blacksmith shop pro-
ducing a variety of 18th-century-
style ironware, specializing in lighting and hardware.*

The Owl's Nest
350 Sparger Road
Mount Airy 27030
(919) 786-7630
*Interpretations and reproductions of
early folk art.*

Pat Scheible
4019 Brookhaven Court
Mebane 27302
(919) 563-3449
*Faux finishes, graining, and
stenciling.*

Philip and Susan Harvey
Route 1, Box 153
Tyner 27980
(919) 221-8425
American country antiques and accessories. Specializes in decoys.

Westmoore Pottery
Route 2, Box 494
Seagrove 27314
(919) 464-3700
Handmade and hand-decorated redware and salt-glazed stoneware pottery made in the tradition and style of the 17th through the 19th century. Mail order.

Willow Oak Antiques
Route 12, Box 3394
Lexington 27232
(919) 764-0192
American country furniture and accessories.

South Carolina

Downtown Antique Mall
217 Main Street
Greenville 29601
(803) 232-6313
Southeastern antiques, collectibles.

Leola Wright
2243 Rifle Range Road
Mount Pleasant 29464
(803) 884-6505
Sweet-grass baskets handwoven by Leola Wright.

Robert M. Hicklin Jr., Inc.
509 East St. John Street
Spartanburg 29302
(803) 583-9847
Fine art and antiques.

Tennessee

Cane Ery Antique Mall
2207 21st Avenue South
Nashville 37212
(615) 269-4780
American primitives, oak furniture, cane and basket supplies, and repair. Mail order.

Carole Wahler Antiques
5209 Green Valley Road
Knoxville 37914
(615) 637-5957
Southern country and primitive furniture, pottery, and baskets. Mail order.

C.B. and Donna Huddleston Antiques
110 Olive Street
Murfreesboro 37130
(615) 890-0932
Country furnishings, accessories, quilts, folk art, and decorative items from the 18th through the 20th century. Mail order.

Cinnamon Hill Antiques
105 High Meadow Drive
Franklin 37064
(615) 790-0833
Formal 18th-century furniture and accessories.

Cumberland General Store
Route 3
Crossville 38555
(615) 484-8481
Old-time mercantile and hardware company carrying kitchen utensils, log-cabin building tools, etc. Mail order.

Henry Teloh Antiques
4302 Sneed Road
Nashville 37215
(615) 292-8886
Cherry and walnut Southern furniture, quilts, coverlets, oriental rugs, and art.

Joy Haley Antiques
3431 Hampton Avenue
Nashville 37215
(615) 297-6364
Country antiques.

Margie Scott, Spring Valley Antiques
4348 Lebanon Road
Hermitage 37076
(615) 889-0267
Country furniture and accessories.

The Murray House
Route 4, Box 312
Northshore Drive
Linair City 37771
(615) 986-4814
American antiques, herbs, and garden supplies.

The Quail's Nest
3422 Springbrook
Nashville 37204
(615) 297-1809
Rag dolls made from antique fabric and other rural Southern accessories. Mail order.

Sandy Arden Antiques
8301 Andersonville Pike
Knoxville 37983
(615) 922-0455
Southern country furniture and accessories. Herbs in season.

Tin Pig Antiques, Inc.
146 Public Square
Lebanon 37087
(615) 444-0072
Antique and country furnishings, collectibles, and accessories.

Virginia

Chequers
University Mall
10635 Braddock Road
Fairfax 22032
(703) 591-2524
Primitive country furniture, folk art, quilts, wreaths, and accessories.

Country Charm
5714 Grove Avenue
"On the Avenues"
Richmond 23226
(804) 285-9696
Pine and oak antique reproduction furniture, rugs, fabric, and accessories. Mail order.

The Country Willow
1510 Pleasure House Road
Virginia Beach 23455
(804) 460-9744
Country furniture, accessories, folk art, quilts, and pottery.

Goose Creek Country
7 Loudon Street SW
Leesburg 22075
(703) 777-6435
Home furnishings and period lighting. Mail order.

H & N Laughon
8106 Three Chopt Road
Richmond 23229
(804) 288-7795
Silhouette artists and historians.

Jenkins-Owen in Virginia
Route 3, Box 230
Hayes 23072
(804) 693-5900
Southern furniture, folk art, and accessories.

Jordan's Country Shop
4080 Foxwood Drive—105
Virginia Beach 23462
(804) 474-2551
Primitive and painted country furniture, folk art, and accessories.

Judith W. Adkins Antiques
230 Lamberth Drive
Danville 24541
(804) 882-2257
Country and Victorian furniture and accessories.

June Lambert
Box 1653
Alexandria 22313
(703) 329-8612
American folk art, textiles, and painted furniture.

Nancy Thomas Studio Gallery
145 Ballard Street
Yorktown 23690
(804) 898-3665
Original art by Thomas, also antiques, quilts, and pottery. Ongoing exhibits by various artists and craftspeople.

Old South Antiques
P.O. Box 44
Brownsburg 24415
(703) 348-5360
American country furniture.

Olde Virginea Floorcloth & Trading Co.
3568 Western Branch Boulevard
P.O. Box 3305
Portsmouth 23707
(804) 397-0948
Handmade floor cloths from 18th-century designs. Custom made. Mail order.

On the Hill
121 Alexander Hamilton Boulevard
P.O. Box 222
Yorktown 23690
(804) 898-3076
Creative arts cooperative of the Yorktown Arts Foundation. Fine arts and crafts made and sold.

Pat Enslin
5128 Hillcrest Lane
Virginia Beach 23464
(804) 495-0410
Original Theorem paintings in traditional themes of plant, animal, home, and legend.

Quilters of Virginia
Route 7, Box 5
Lexington 24450
(703) 463-4636
Handmade quilts in contemporary designs.

Sandi Wickersham Resnick
P.O. Box 958
Purcellville 22132
(703) 338-9503
American primitive artist. Original paintings and lithographs depicting country life. Mail order.

Shaia Oriental Rugs of Williamsburg
501 Prince George Street
Williamsburg 23185
(804) 220-0400
Antique, semi-antique, and new oriental rugs.

Wonderful Things
On the Green at the Boar's Head Inn
Charlottesville 22901
(804) 296-8379
Crafts and decorative items.

Washington, D.C.

Cherishables
1608 20 Street NW
Washington 20009
18th- and 19th-century American furniture, folk art, and quilts. Mail order.

Marston Luce Antiques
1314 21 Street
Washington 20036
(202) 775-9460
American 19th-century cast-iron furniture and decorations; painted furniture, weather vanes, quilts, and architectural elements.

Nancy J. Campbell, Antiques
1214 31 Street NW
Washington 20007
(202) 333-8448
Fine antiques and works of art. Unusual birdcages—large and small.

The Old Print Gallery
1220 31st Street NW
Washington 20007
(202) 965-1818
Original antique prints and maps, including historical scenes and portraits, town views, and natural history. Mail-order catalog available.

Patricia Smith's Quilts, Etc.
3707 Woodley Road NW
Washington 20016
(202) 244-0859
Quilts made prior to 1940, all types. Mail order.

Taggart and Jorgensen Gallery
3241 P Street NW
Washington 20007
(202) 298-7676
Specialists in 19th- and early 20th-century American paintings.

Wickens and Hicks American Store
1455 Pennsylvania Avenue
Washington, D.C. 20004
(202) 347-8880
A variety of herb plants and topiaries, as well as new and antique linens. Hand-painted dinnerware also available.

Directory of Museums and Historic Sites

Alabama

The Fine Arts Museum of the
   South
Museum Drive
Mobile 36608
(205) 342-4642
*Southern decorative art from early
to mid-19th century.*

Florida

Bonnet House
Florida Trust for Historic
   Preservation
900 North Birch Road
Fort Lauderdale 33304
(305) 563-5393
*Home of Frederick Clay Bartlett
and Evelyn Fortune Bartlett. Tours
scheduled by reservation only.*

Thomas Edison Home
2350 McGregor Boulevard
Fort Myers 33901
(813) 334-3614
*Thomas Edison's winter home, now
a museum. Open Monday to Saturday, 9:00 A.M. to 4:00 P.M., Sunday, 12:30 to 4:00 P.M.*

The Wrecker's Museum (The
   Oldest House in Key West)
322 Duval Street
Key West 33040
(305) 294-1589
*Home of Francis Watlington, a li-
censed salvager of shipwrecks. Built
to resemble the hull of a ship, the
house is furnished to show the life-
style in the Key West of 1830 to
1880. Open seven days a week
from 10:00 A.M. to 4:00 P.M.*

Kentucky

Shaker Village at Pleasant Hill
3500 Lexington Road
Harrodsburg 40330
(606) 734-5411
*Historic preservation of 19th-
century Shaker village; includes
costumed guides reenacting
Shaker crafts.*

Mississippi

Balfour House
1002 Crawford Street
P.O. Box 1541
Vicksburg 39180
(601) 638-3690

The Grand Village of the Natchez
   Indians
400 Jefferson Davis Boulevard
Natchez 39120
(601) 446-6502
*Location of the historic ceremonial
mound center of the Natchez tribe.
The site features a museum, nature
trails, and a reconstructed Natchez
house.*

North Carolina

Historic Edenton
P.O. Box 474
Edenton 27932
(919) 482-2637
(919) 482-3663
*The first capital of the province of
North Carolina. Several architec-
tural styles.*

Museum of Early Southern
   Decorative Arts
924 South Main Street
P.O. Box 10310
Winston-Salem 27108
(919) 721-7300
*Nineteenth-century period
rooms, with furniture and objects
made and used in the South
through 1820.*

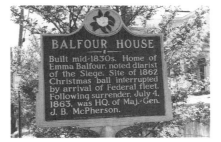

North Carolina

Old Salem
Old Salem Road
Drawer F, Salem Station
Winston-Salem 27108
(919) 723-3688
*Restored Moravian village of the
18th and 19th centuries.*

South Carolina

Middleton Place
Ashley River Road
Charleston 29414
(803) 556-6020
*An early 19th-century rice planta-
tion and landscaped gardens.*

Walnut Grove Plantation
1200 Ott's Shoals Road
Roebuck 29376
(803) 576-6546
*Built in the late 18th century,
this plantation house portrays life
in pre-1830 America.*

Tennessee

James K. Polk Ancestral Home
301 West 7th Street
P.O. Box 741
Columbia 38402
(615) 388-2354
This restored 1816 Federal-style house was once the home of President James K. Polk. The collection includes possessions of President and Mrs. Polk, as well as related documentary artifacts.

Virginia

Colonial Williamsburg
P.O. Box C
Williamsburg 23185
(800) 447-8679
Re-created 18th-century colonial village with shops, houses, public buildings, and gardens.

Westover Plantation
Route 2, Box 445
Charles City 23030
(804) 795-2882
Built about 1730 by William Bird II. The grounds and garden are open to the public.

Woodlawn Plantation
P.O. Box 37
Mount Vernon 22121
(703) 780-4000
Restored home of Nelly Custis Lewis, Martha Washington's granddaughter. Nineteenth-century plantation house designed by Dr. William Thornton, first architect of the U.S. Capitol.

Washington, D.C.

Old Stone House
3051 M Street NW
Washington 20007
(202) 426-6851 (voice or TDD)
The oldest stone structure in the District of Columbia, built in 1765 by Christopher Layman. Open Wednesday to Sunday, 9:30 A.M. to 5:00 P.M. Closed Monday and Tuesday.

Directory of Food Sources

Alabama

Joe Williams Pecans
P.O. Box 640
Camden 36726
Shelled pecans, whole halves or large pieces, available from November through August.

Florida

Albriton Fruit Company, Inc.
5430 Procter Road
Sarasota 33583
(813) 923-2573
Citrus fruit and specialties, as well as mangoes and avocados.

Barfield Groves
P.O. Box 68
Polk City 33868
(813) 984-1316
Fresh Florida citrus fruit

Blue Heron Fruit Shippers
7440 North Trail
Sarasota 33580
(813) 355-6946
Fresh oranges, grapefruit, mangoes, and avocados

Chalet Suzanne Foods, Inc.
E.O. Drawer AC
Lake Wales 33859
(813) 676-6011
Gourmet soups, sauces, and aspics.

Lee's Fruit Company
P.O. Box 2801
Leesburg 32748
(904) 753-0555
Organic fruit, plant food, and compost.

Qualil Roost Quail Farms, Inc.
8942 SW 129 Terrace
Miami 33176
(305) 253-8319
Fresh dressed and frozen quail and pheasant.

St. James
P.O. Box 222800
Hollywood 33022-2800
(305) 921-8882
Wisconsin cheddars aged a minimum of two years.

Georgia

Exotica Brands, Inc.
P.O. Box 450134
Atlanta 30345
(404) 496-0731
Brauhaus Beer Bread Mixes and a variety of bread mixes made without beer, such as Coa Bread and Yogurt Herb Bread.
   Send a self-addressed, stamped envelope for a free brochure.

Koinonia Products
Route 2
Americus 31709
(912) 924-0391

Shelled, hand-sorted pecan halves and pieces, pecan specialty items, fruitcake, and peanuts.

Southern Cross Farms
P.O. Box 627
Vidalia 30474
(912) 565-7880
Out of state: (800) 833-0009
Vidalia sweet onions and specialty foods, including pecans and sweet potatoes.

Kentucky

Gethsemani Farms
Highway 247
Trappist 40051
(502) 549-3117
Cheese and fruitcakes.

Louisiana

Bayou Buffet
P.O. Box 791127
New Orleans 70179-1127
(504) 482-3752
Creole and Cajun seasonings, mixes, cookbooks, and kitchen equipment.

Bayou Food Products
1915 North Main Street
Saint Martinville 70582
(318) 394-5552
Cajun ethnic items unique to the St. Martinville area, including hot sauces, pickled peppers, okra, spices, and recipes.

Calhoun Pecan Shelling
   Company
P.O. Box 784, Dept. ACC
Mansfield 71052
(318) 872-2921

Fancy shelled pecan halves and cooking pieces in economy packs and decorative tins.

Community Kitchens
P.O. Box 3778
Baton Rouge 70821-3778
Out of state: (800) 535-9901
Special coffee blends of the region, Cajun spices, Creole seasonings, mixes, and gourmet teas.

Evangeline Foods
P.O. Box 798
Banker Rd.
Saint Martinville 70582
(318) 394-3091
Hot sauces, pickled peppers, pepper sauces, long- and medium-grain rice, and Regent and Chinito brand rice.

Gazin's
2910 Toulouse Street
P.O. Box 19221
New Orleans 70179
(504) 482-0302
Creole and Cajun foods and spices. Catalog $1, refundable with first order.

Zatarain's, Inc.
82 First Street
P.O. Box 347
Gretna 70053
(504) 367-2950
Breading, seasonings, and Creole specialties.

Maryland

Big Al's Seafood Market
302 Talbot Street
Saint Michaels 21663
(301) 745-2637
Big Al's own crab seasoning mix.

Custard Company
4877 Battery Lane, #32
Bethesda 20814
(301) 652-9141
Coffee cakes and brownies made without preservatives, artificial colorings, or artificial flavorings.

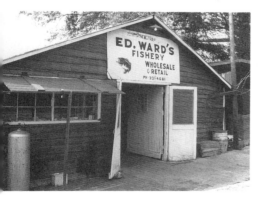

Roy L. Hoffman & Sons
Route 6, Box 5
Hagerstown 21740
(301) 739-2332
Country ham and bacon, smoked turkey, steaks, smoked pork chops, and smoked summer sausages.

Mississippi

Sternberg Pecan Company
P.O. Box 193
Jackson 39205
(601) 366-6310
Direct-mail sales of fresh, shelled, fancy mammoth pecan halves.

North Carolina

Maria's
111 Stratford Road
Winston-Salem 27104
(919) 722-7271
Fresh coffees roasted daily. Also a complete line of bulk spices and herbs, teas, fruits, nuts, cheeses, specialty foods, and gift baskets. Free catalog.

South Carolina

Eugene Platt's Fish Company
Atlantis Sturgeon Caviar
    Department
714 Sea Mountain Highway
North Myrtle Beach 29582
(803) 249-3711
(803) 249-2008
Fresh Atlantic sturgeon caviar.

Maurice's Gourmet Barbecue
P.O. Box 6847
West Columbia 29171
Out of state: (800) 628-7423
Special barbecue sauces and spices.

Nuts D'Vine
P.O. Box 589
Edenton 27932
(919) 482-2222
Out of state: (800) 334-0492
Gourmet peanuts in the shell, shelled, and water-blanched. True cold-pressed virgin peanut oil also available.

Virginia

Fabulous Foodstuffs
1234 First Street
Department BK
Alexandria 22314
(703) 836-5005
French butter, Parmesan, cheddar, and other natural cheeses.

Gwaltney of Smithfield Ltd.
P.O. Box 489
Smithfield 23430
(804) 357-3131
Cured and smoked Smithfield and Williamsburg brand hams, bacon, sausages, luncheon meats, franks, and fresh pork.

R & R Limited of Smithfield
124 Main Street
P.O. Box 837
Smithfield 23430
(804) 357-5730
Smithfield hams and bacon, Virginia peanuts and preserves, and selected gift items.

Smithfield Packing Co.
P.O. Box 447
Smithfield 23430
(804) 357-4321
Genuine Smithfield hams and country-cured hams and bacon. Hams are sold either cooked or uncooked.

Summerfield Farm Products Ltd.
Route 1, Box 43
Boyce 22620
(703) 837-1718
Producers of true milk-fed veal. Baby spring lambs and free-range chickens are also available.

S. Wallace Edwards & Sons, Inc.
P.O. Box 25
Surry 23883
(804) 294-3121
Out of state: (800) 222-4267
Genuine cured Virginia hams, bacon, and sausages.
    Write or call for free brochure.

Teel Mountain Farm
Route 1, Box 411
Stanardsville 22973
(804) 985-7608
Natural organic whole chickens and chicken parts.

V. W. Joyner and Company
315 Main Street
Smithfield 23430
Out of state: (800) 628-2242
Smithfield hams and smoked meats.

Index